THE BLACK KEYS
A COLLECTION

CONTENTS

This book was approved by The Black Keys

Photo Credit John Peets

Transcribed by Steve Gorenberg and Jeff Jacobson

Cherry Lane Music Company
Director of Publications/Project Editor: Mark Phillips
Project Coordinator: Rebecca Skidmore

ISBN 978-1-60378-229-6

Visit our website at www.cherrylaneprint.com

10 A.M. AUTOMATIC

Words and Music by
Dan Auerbach and Patrick Carney

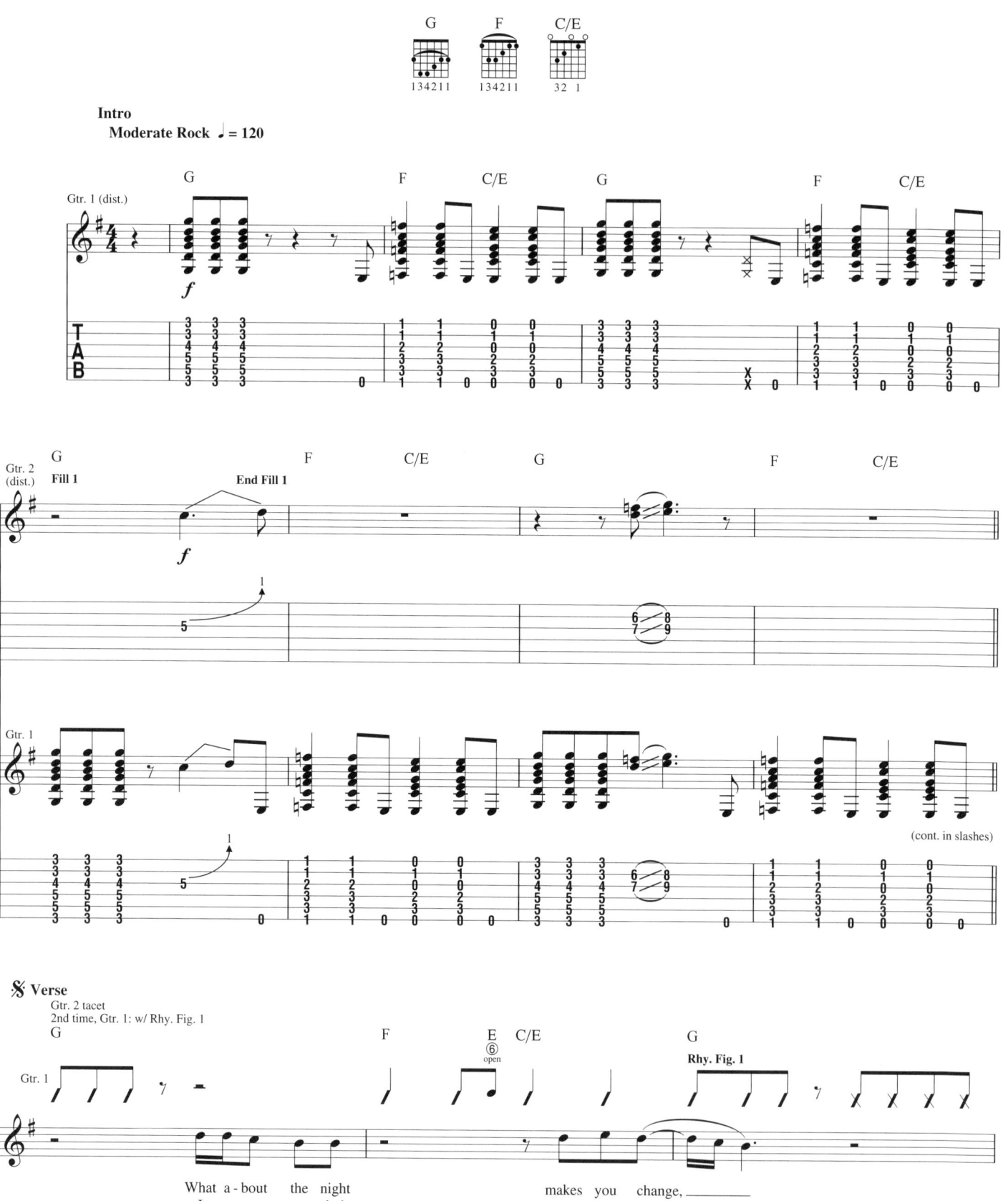

3

Chorus

2nd time, Gtr. 2: w/ Fill 4

(1st time) Yeah.

Gtr. 1: w/ Riff A (1 1/2 times)
1st time, Gtr. 2: w/ Riff A1 (2 times)

2nd time, Gtr. 2: w/ Riff A1 (last 3 meas.)

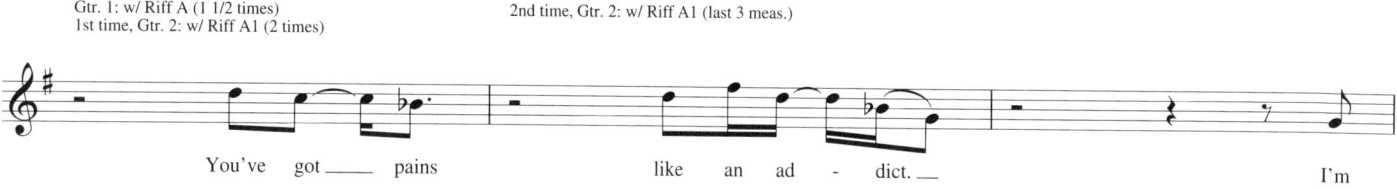

You've got _____ pains   like an ad - dict. _____   I'm

2nd time, Gtr. 2: w/ Riff A1 (1st 3 meas.)

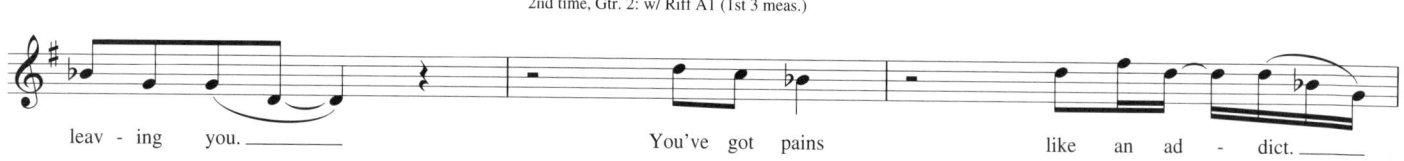

leav - ing you. _____   You've got pains   like an ad - dict. _____

4

5

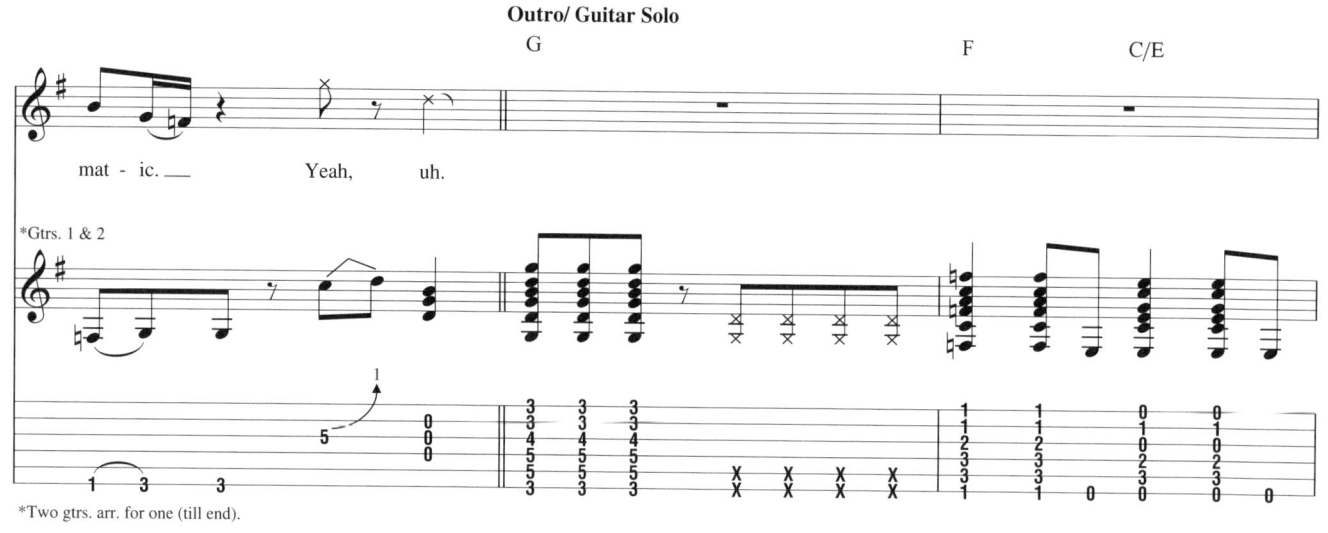

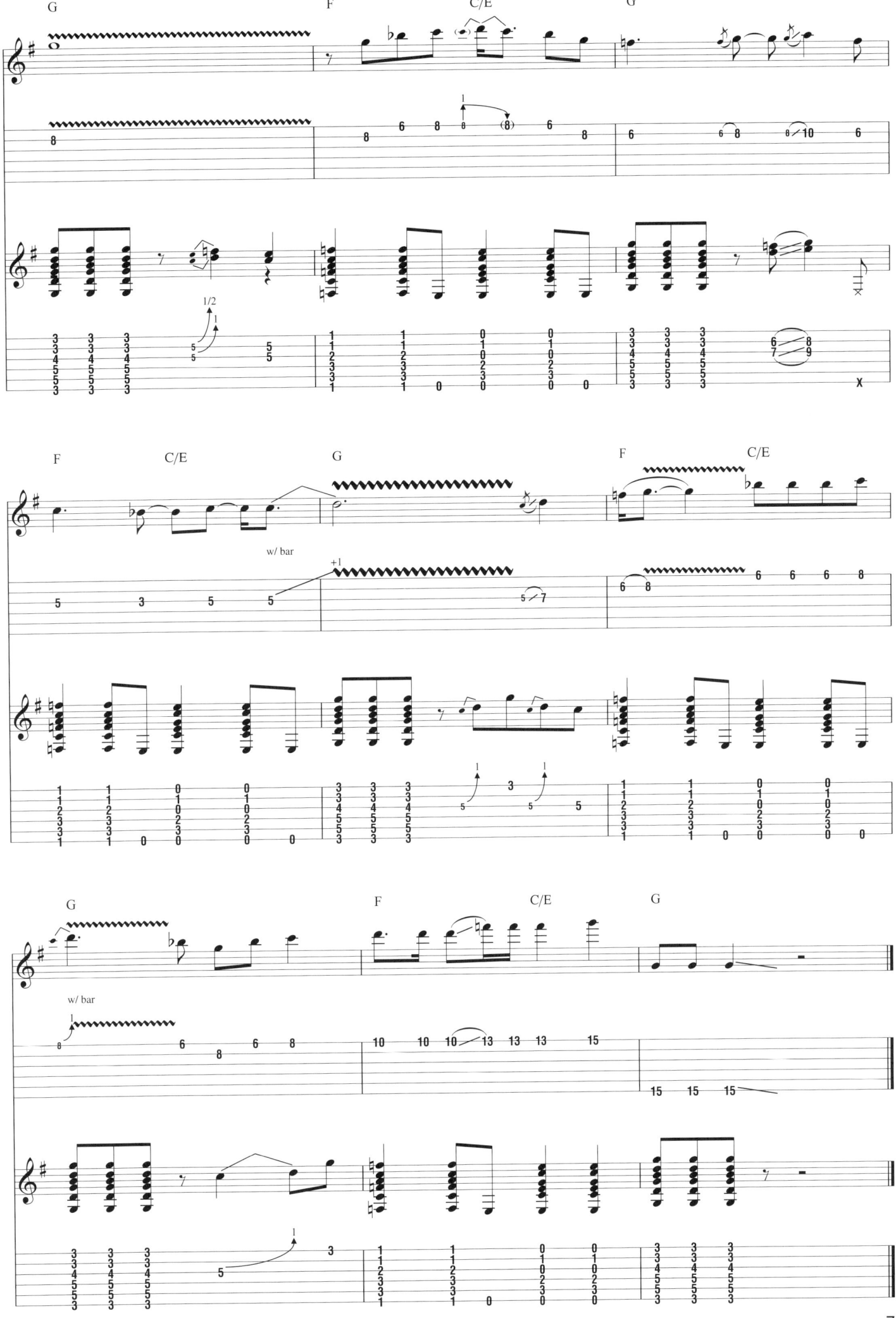

GIRL IS ON MY MIND

Words and Music by
Dan Auerbach and Patrick Carney

*Capo II

Intro
Moderate Rock ♩ = 112

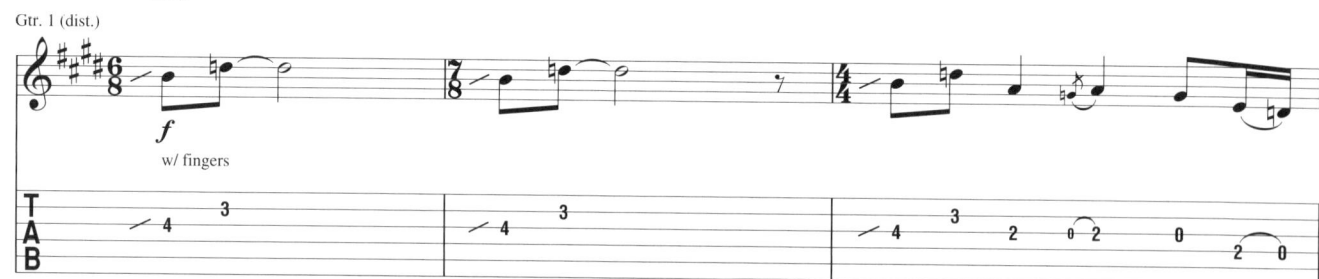

*All music sounds a whole step higher than indicated due to capo.

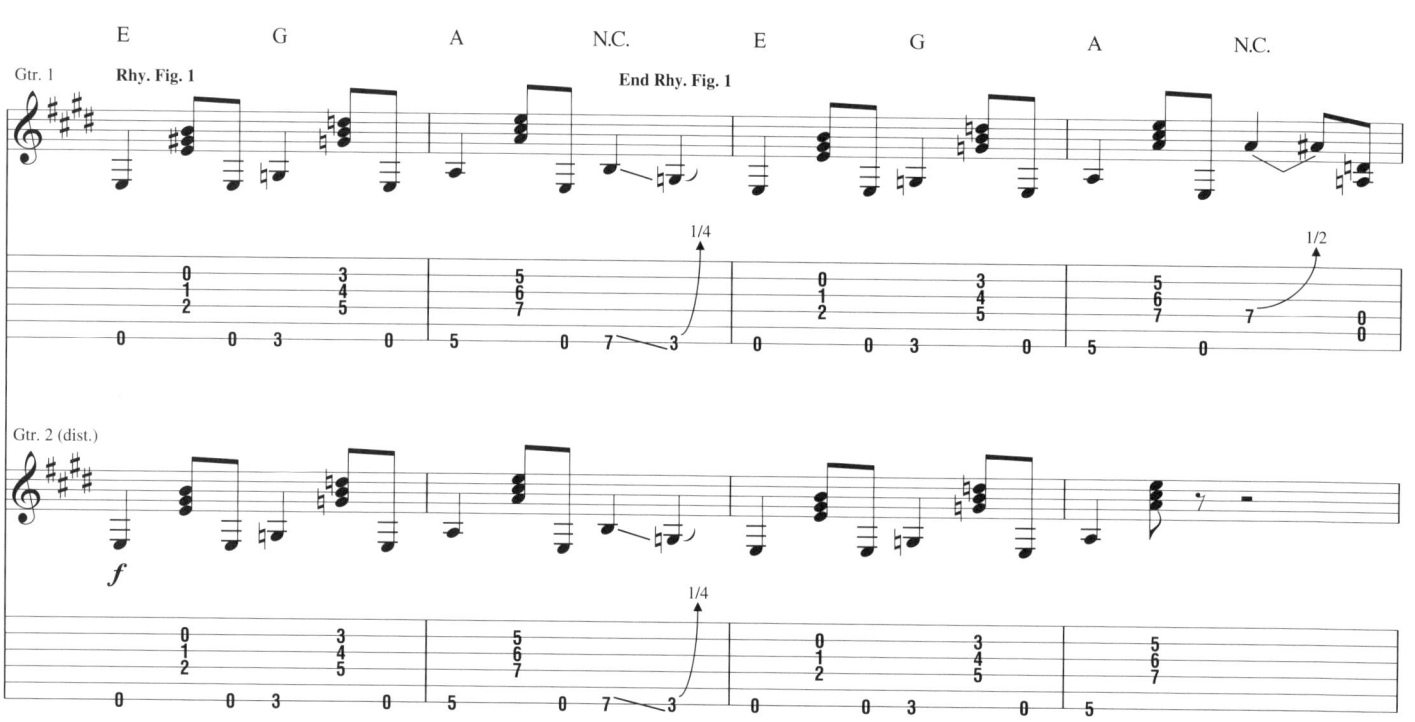

Gtr. 2: w/ Rhy. Fig. 1 (2 times)

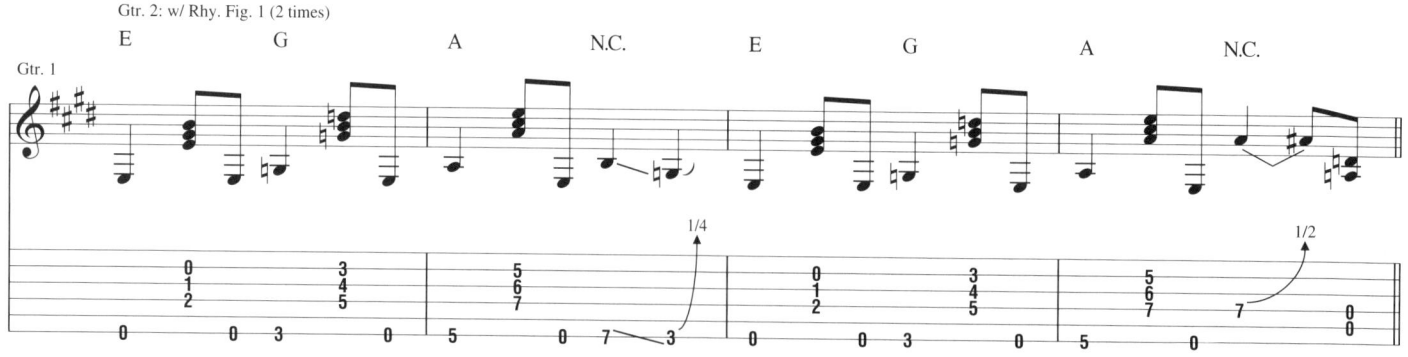

Copyright © 2004 McMoore McLesst Publishing (BMI)
All Rights in the world excluding Australia and New Zealand Administered by Wixen Music Publishing, Inc.
All Rights in Australia and New Zealand Administered by GaGa Music
All Rights Reserved   Used by Permission

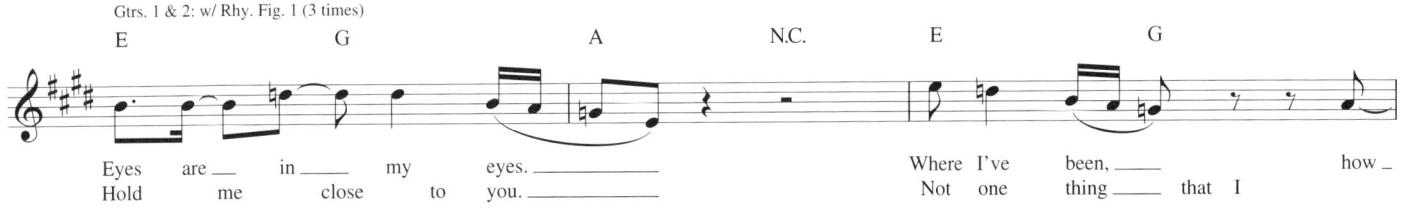

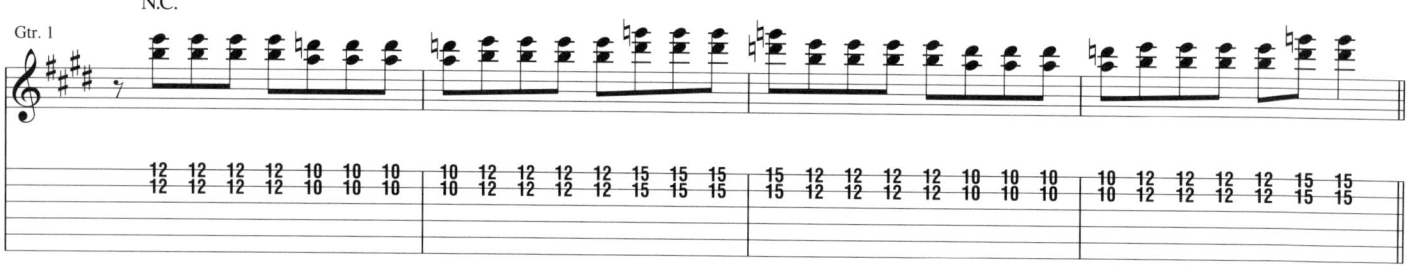

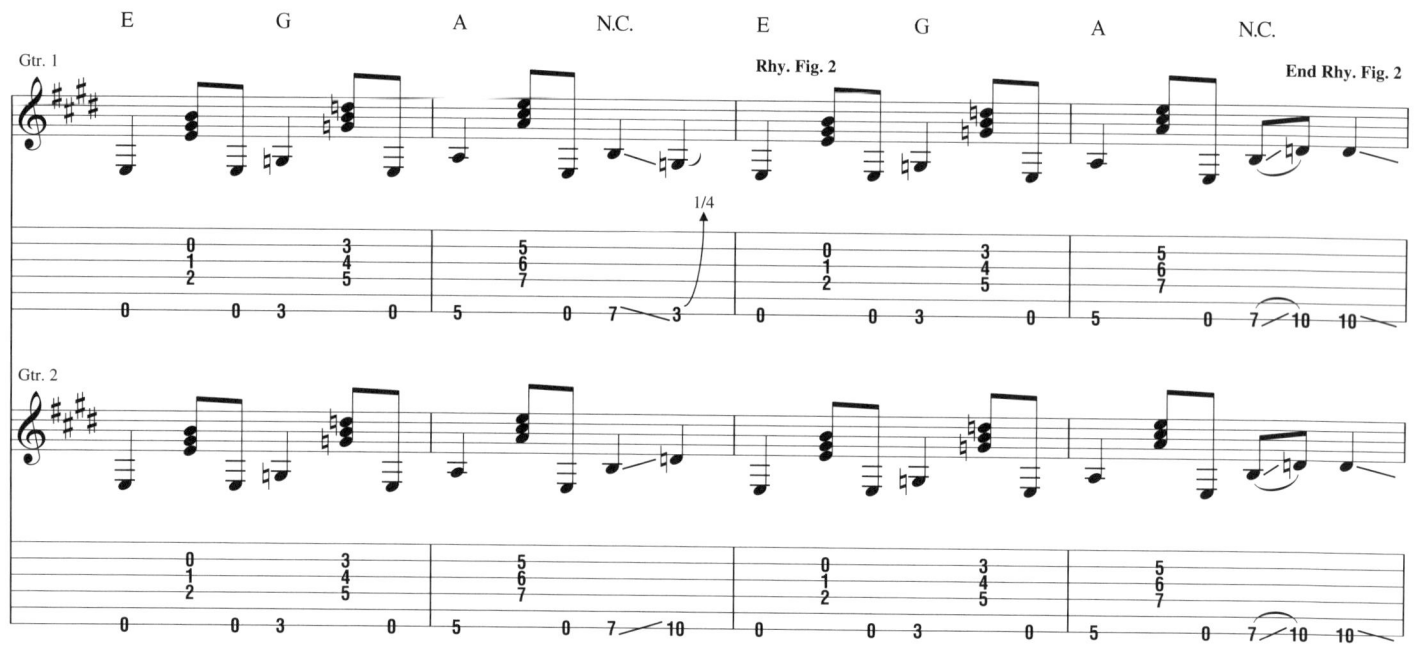

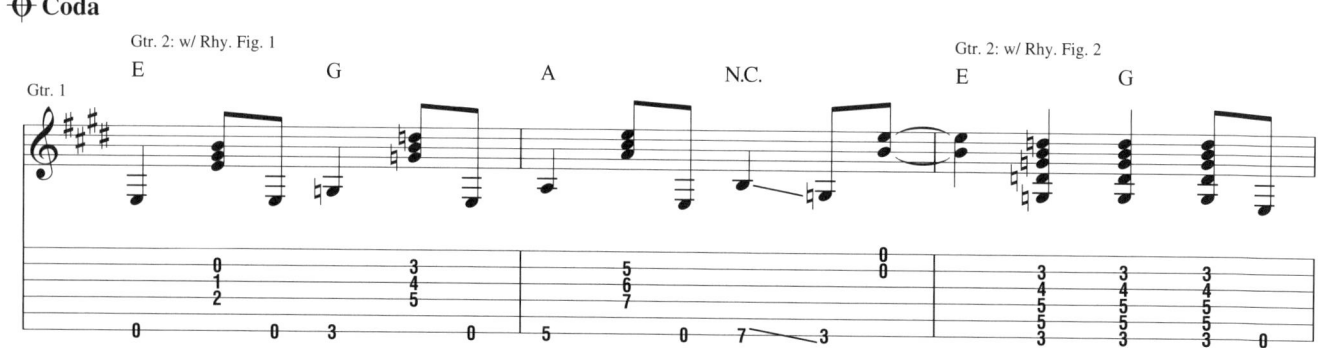

Guitar Solo

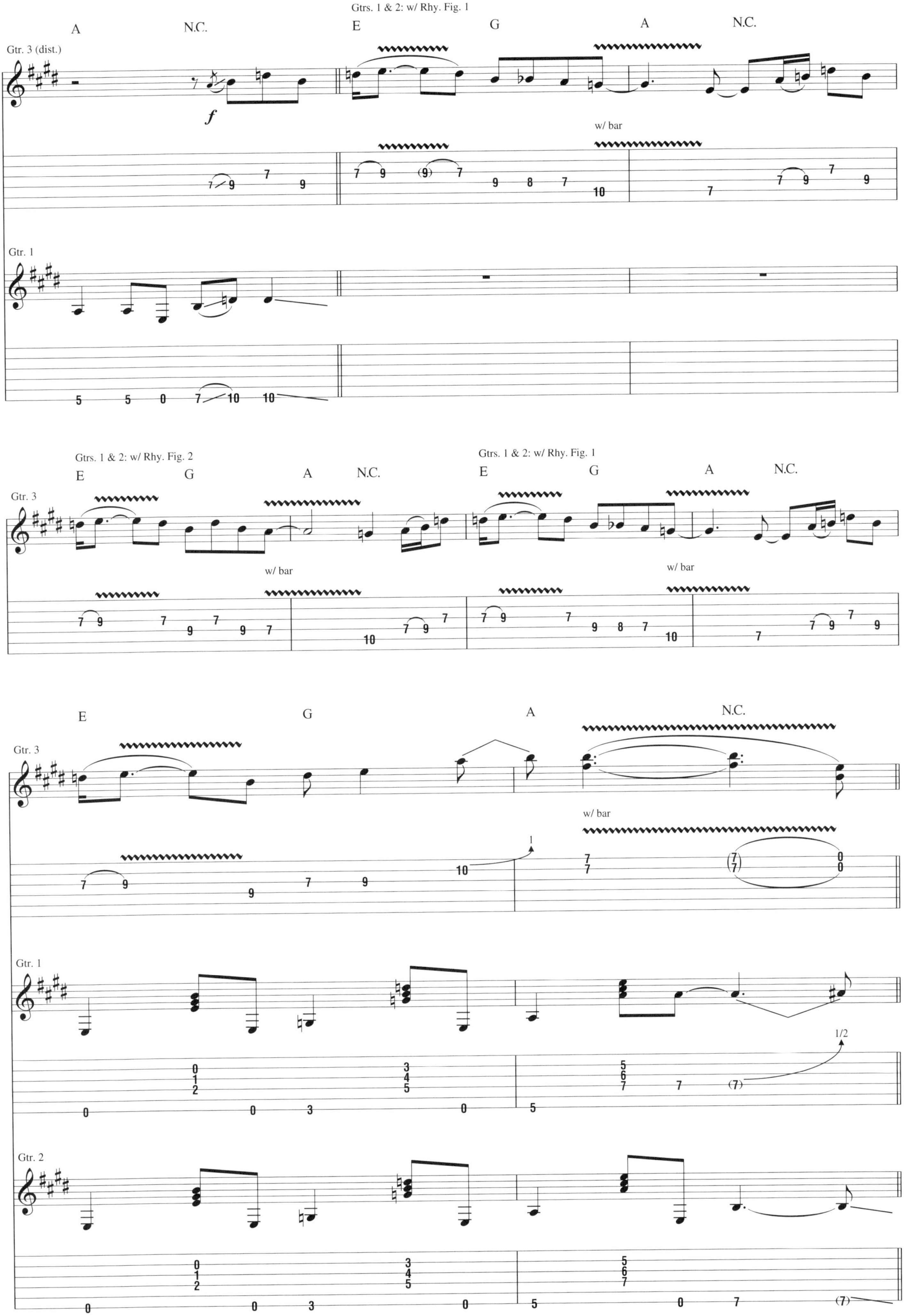
Gtrs. 1 & 2: w/ Rhy. Fig. 1
A
N.C.
E
G
A
N.C.
Gtr. 3 (dist.)
f
w/ bar
Gtr. 1
Gtrs. 1 & 2: w/ Rhy. Fig. 2
E
G
A
N.C.
Gtrs. 1 & 2: w/ Rhy. Fig. 1
E
G
A
N.C.
Gtr. 3
w/ bar
w/ bar
E
G
A
N.C.
Gtr. 3
w/ bar
1
Gtr. 1
1/2
Gtr. 2

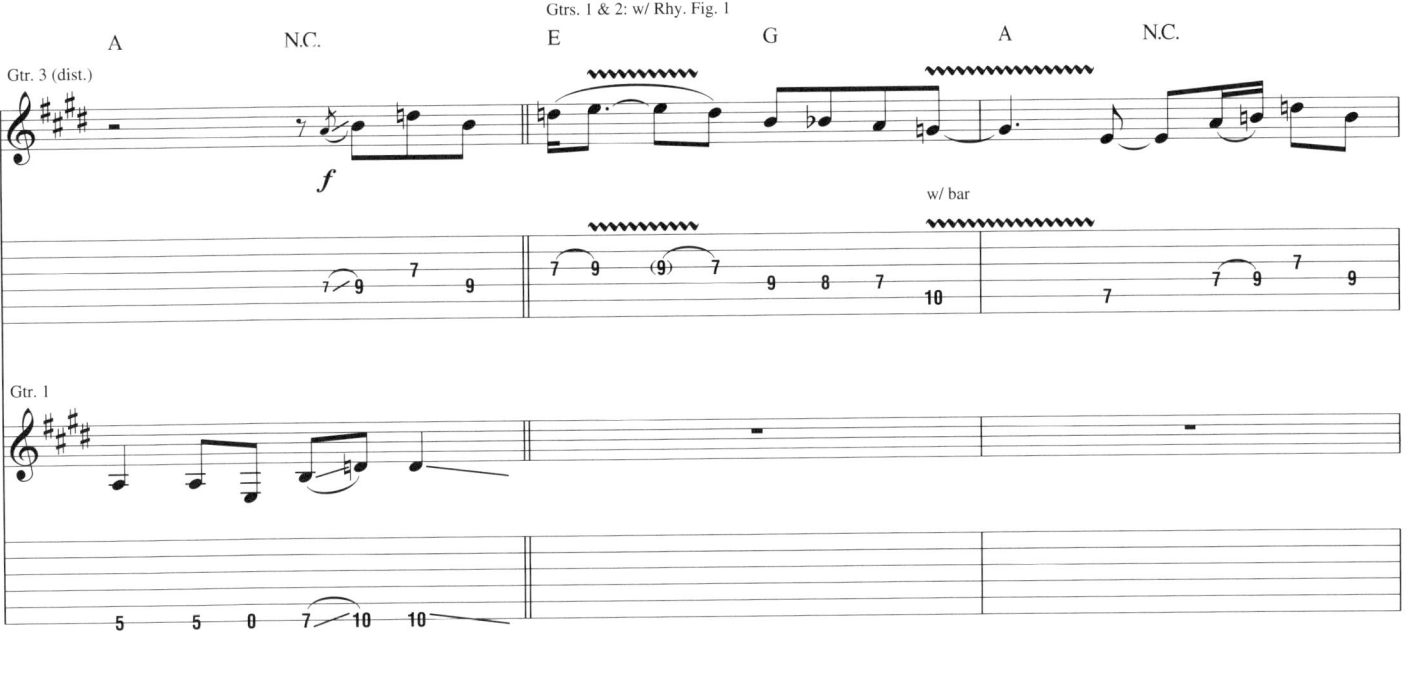

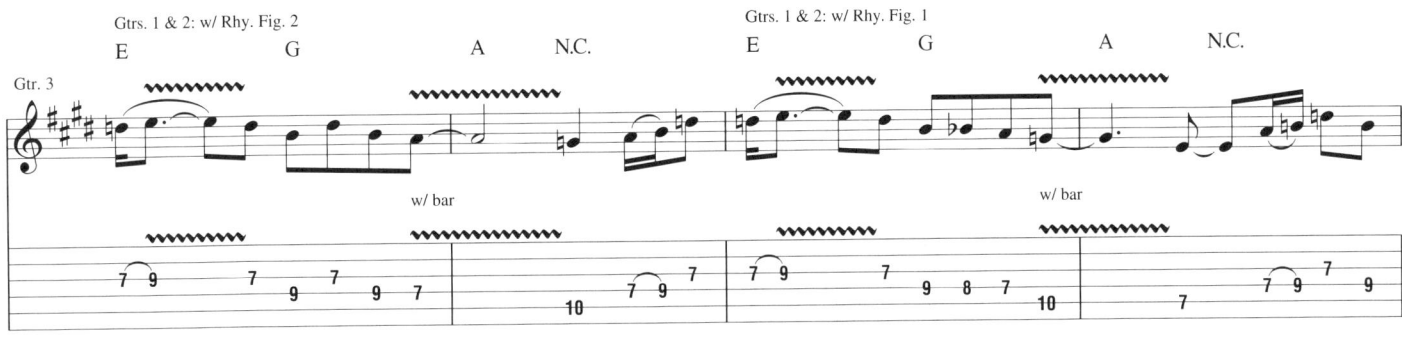

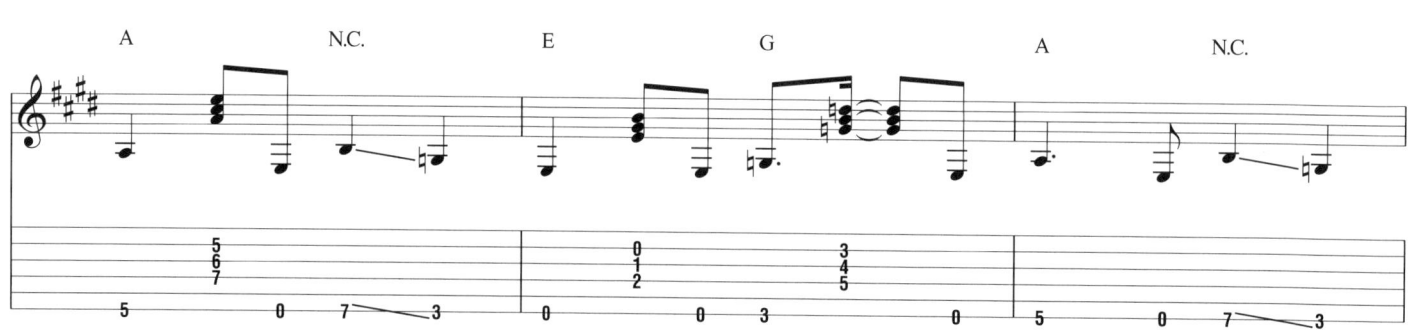

3. Girl is on _____ my mind. _

She is on _____ my mind. _

Try to ig - nore, ____ try to un - wind; ____ she is on ____ my mind. __

Outro

Oo. ____

Oo, _____ oo. Oo. ____

let ring - - - - - - -   *let ring - - - - - - -*

let ring - - - -   *let ring - - - - -*   *let ring - - - - -*   *let ring - - - - -*

GOODBYE BABYLON

Words and Music by
Dan Auerbach and Patrick Carney

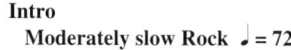

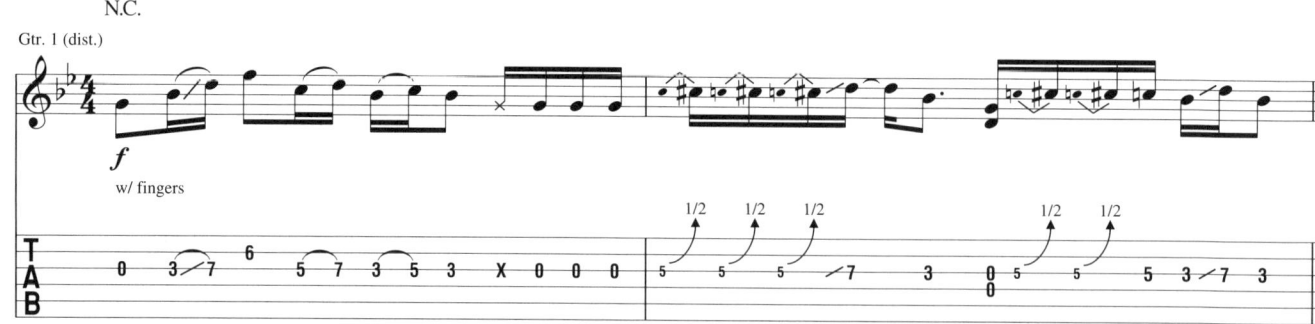

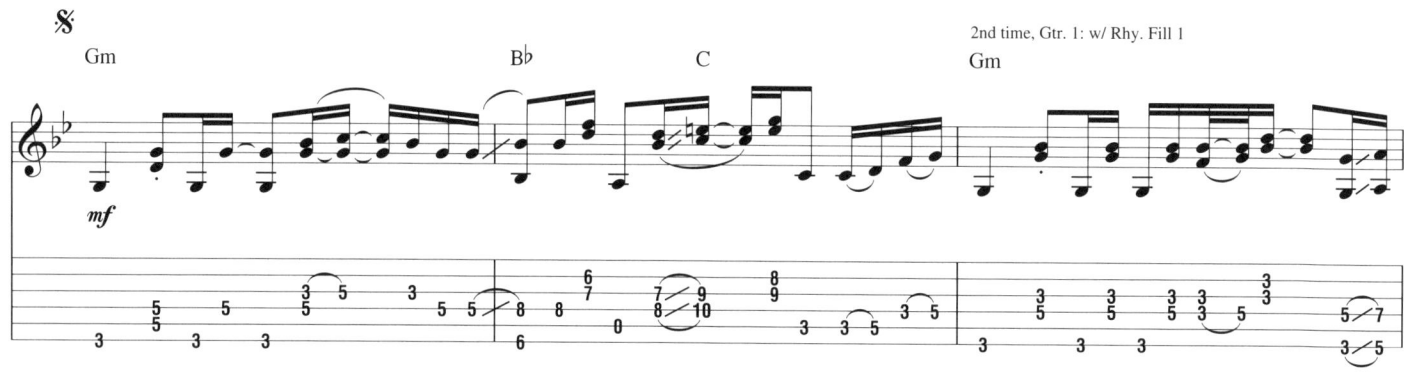

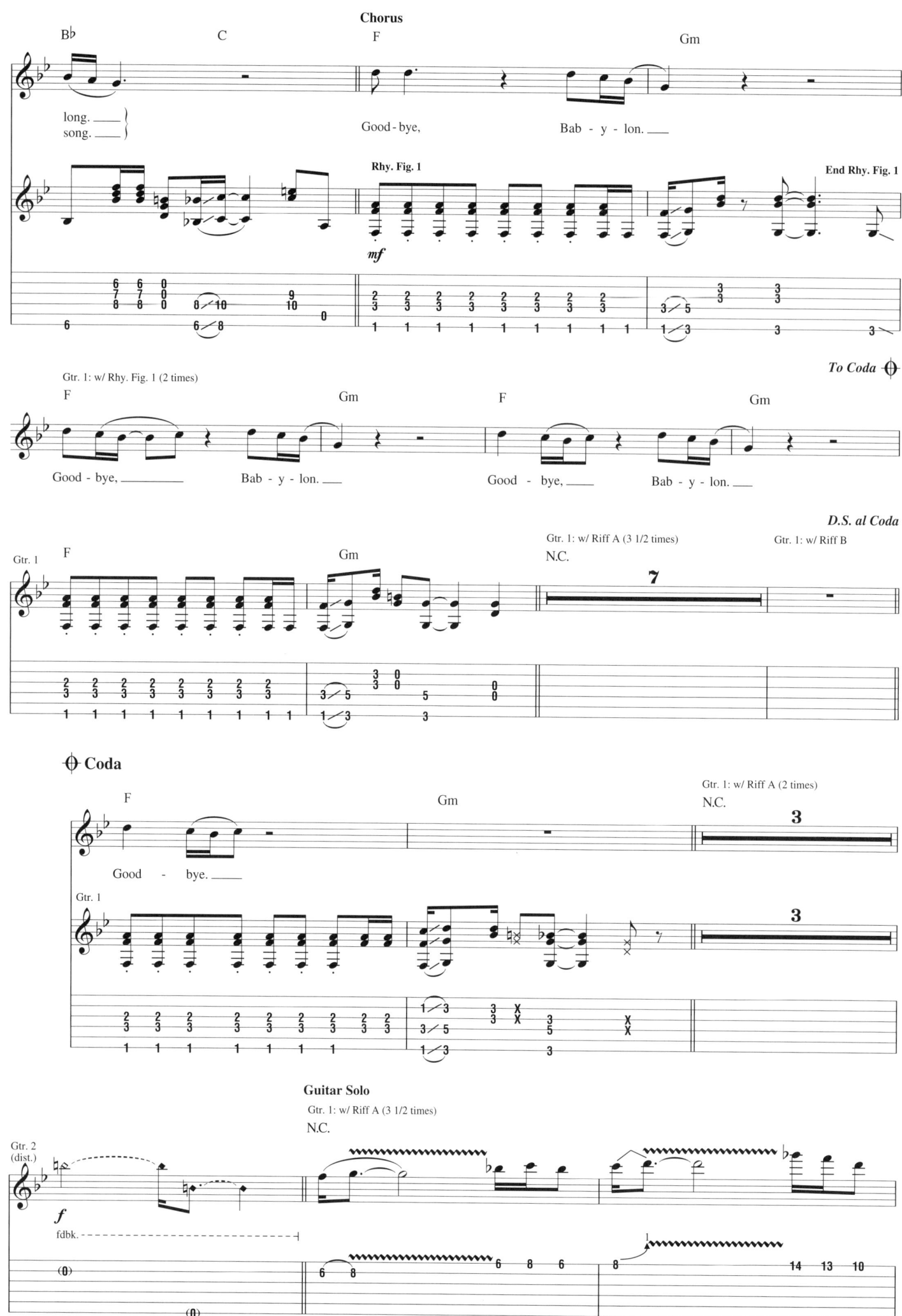

Chorus

long. ___ } song. ___ }

Good - bye, Bab - y - lon. ___

Rhy. Fig. 1   **End Rhy. Fig. 1**

mf

Gtr. 1: w/ Rhy. Fig. 1 (2 times)

Good - bye, ___ Bab - y - lon. ___ Good - bye, ___ Bab - y - lon. ___

To Coda ⊕

D.S. al Coda

Gtr. 1: w/ Riff A (3 1/2 times)   Gtr. 1: w/ Riff B

Gtr. 1   N.C.

⊕ **Coda**

Gtr. 1: w/ Riff A (2 times)

Good - bye. ___

Gtr. 1

Guitar Solo

Gtr. 1: w/ Riff A (3 1/2 times)

N.C.

Gtr. 2 (dist.)

f

fdbk. - - - - -

Pitch: B

16

Gtr. 1: w/ Riff B

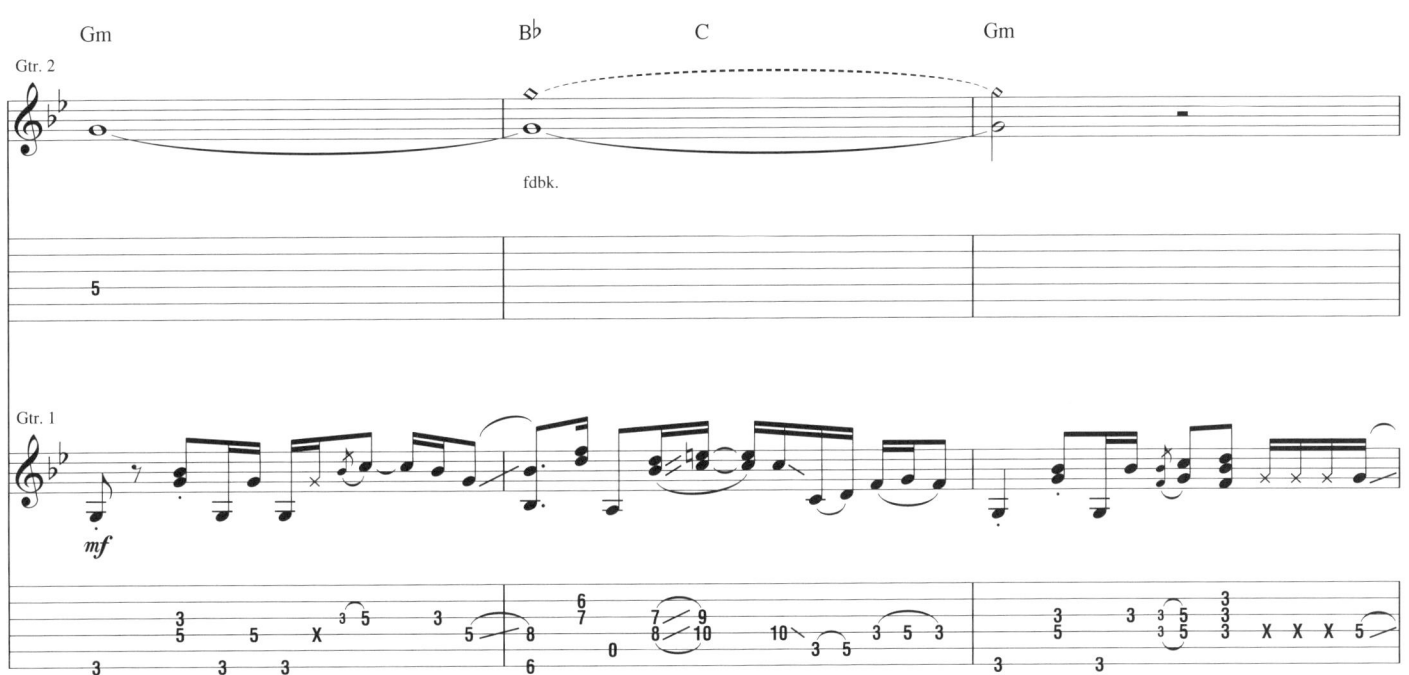

Verse

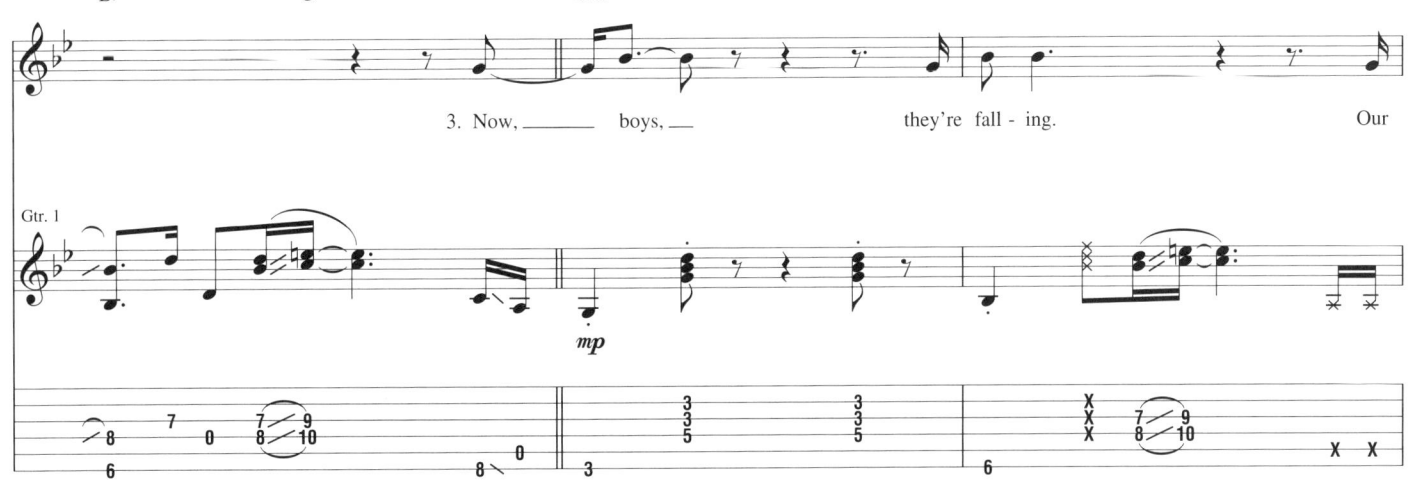

3. Now, _____ boys, ___ they're fall - ing. Our

17

Chorus

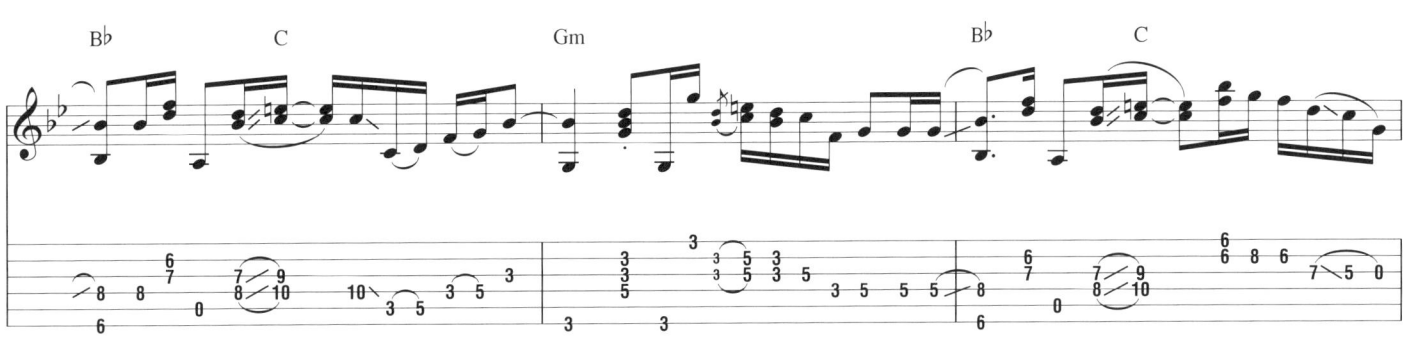

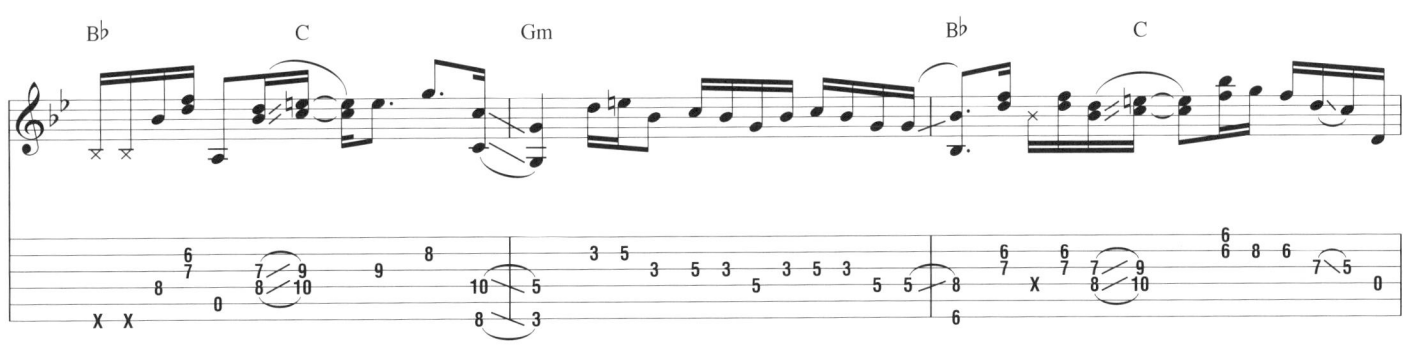

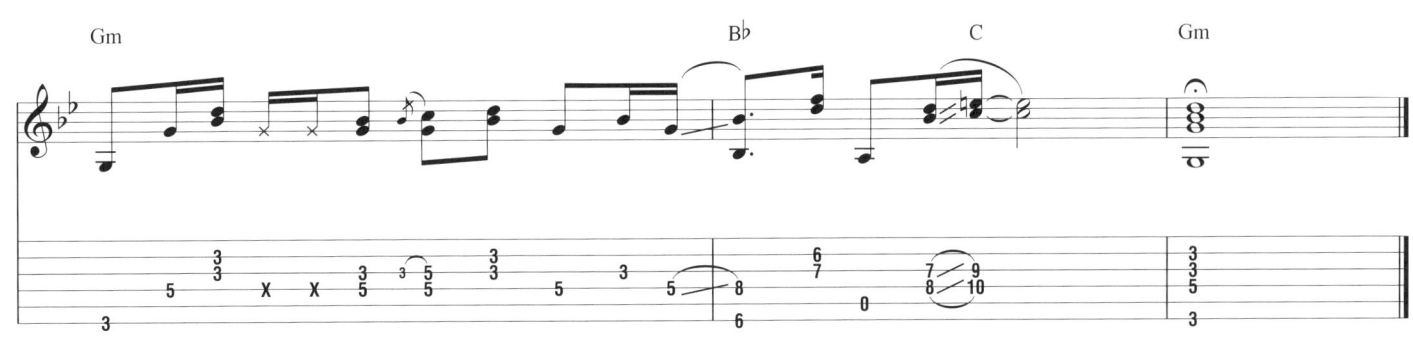

HARD ROW

Words and Music by
Dan Auerbach, Patrick Carney
and Chuck Auerbach

20

Chorus

night gets dark, all is still. ___ You pray for me, _____ I

know you will. ___ Hard row to hoe _____ all by ___ your-

self.
(Sing 1st time only)

2. We hit the cit-

𝄋 Verse

y; _____ yeah. ___
Walk out on him. ___

it swal-low you whole. ___

Fill 1
Gtr. 2

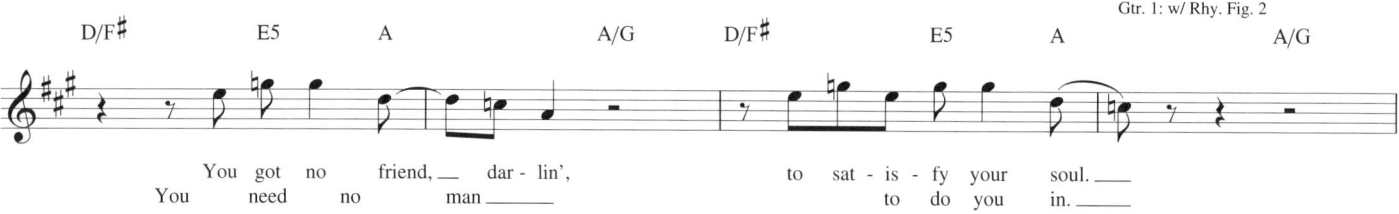

You got no friend, __ dar - lin', to sat - is - fy your soul. __
You need no man _____ to do you in. __

Chorus

And then the side - walk ends, __ lights __ all red. __
But if the night gets dark, __ all is still, __ I'll

Say to your - self, __ bet - ter off dead. __
pray for you. __ You know I will.

Hard row to hoe __

To Coda

__ all by _____ your - self.

(Sing 1st time only)

Interlude

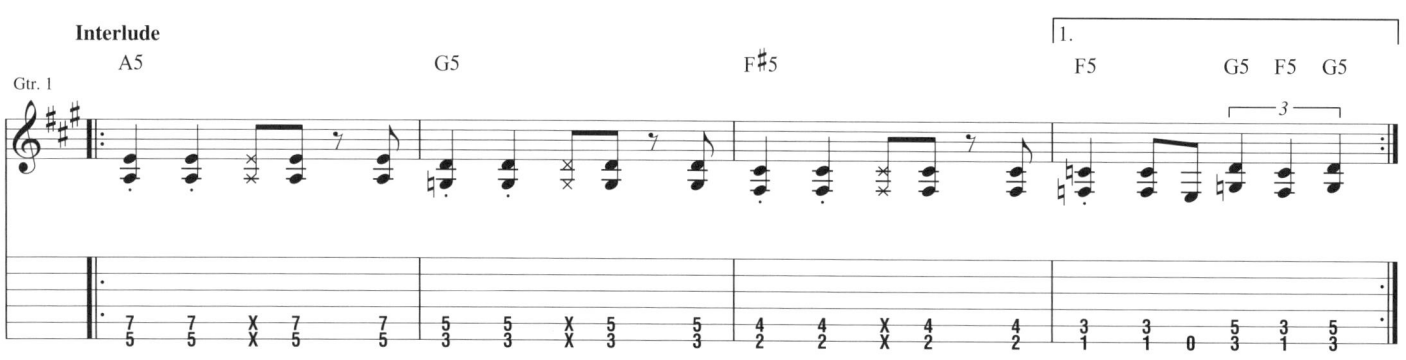

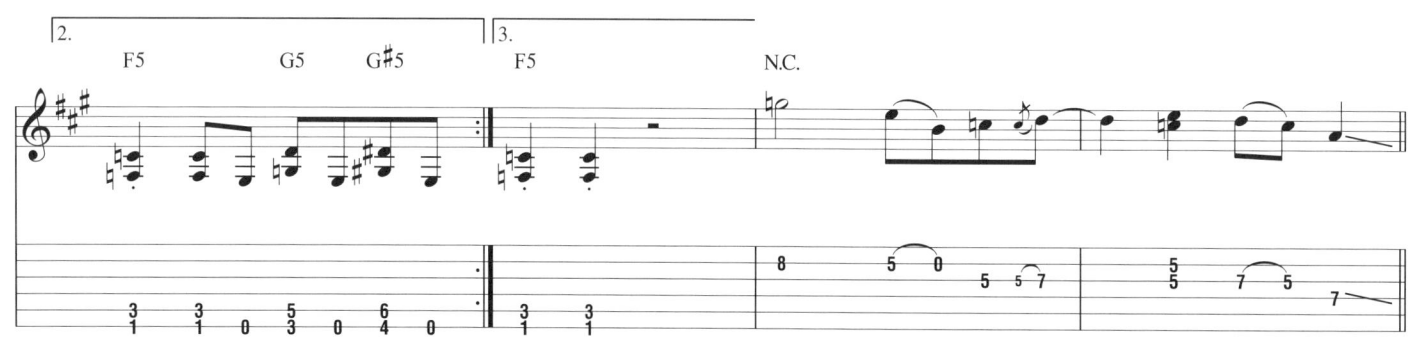

22

Guitar Solo

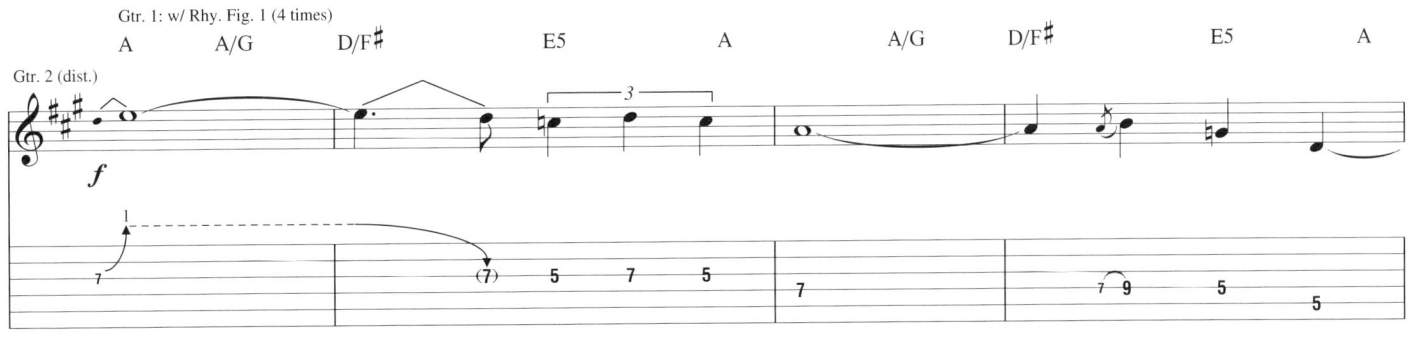

Coda

I GOT MINE

Words and Music by
Dan Auerbach and Patrick Carney

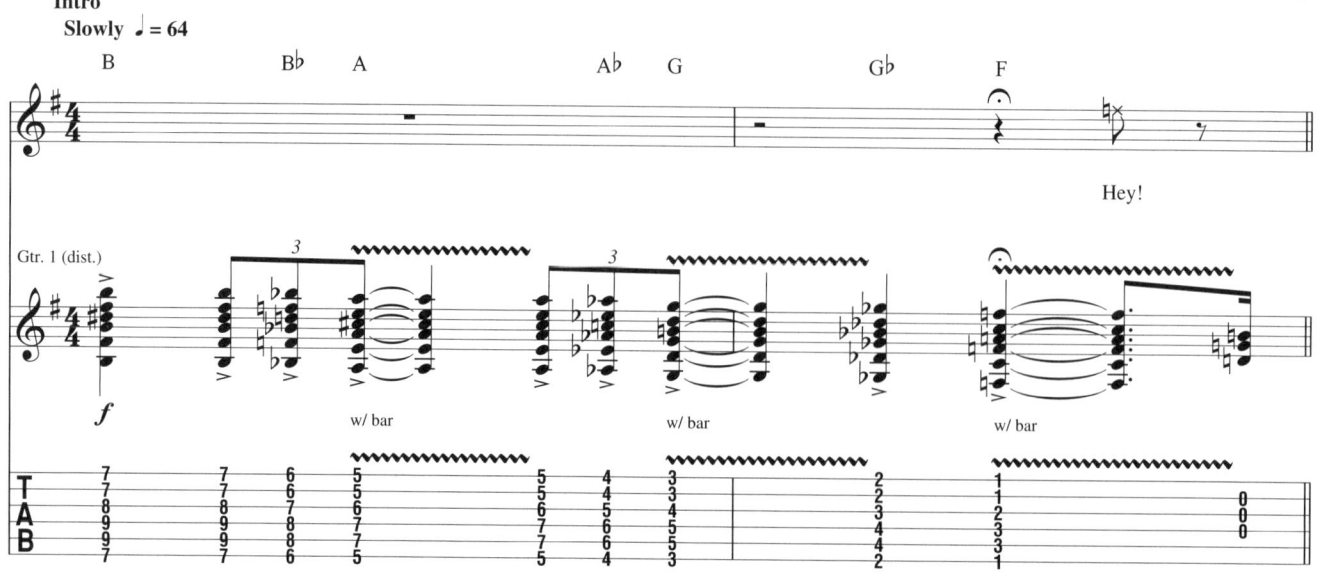

24

Verse

in my young - er days. But I've grown out of my ram - blin' ways. I left that road, ah, so far be - hind. And now I know, oh, ba - by, I got mine.

slight P.M.

*T = Thumb on 6th string.

cresc.

25

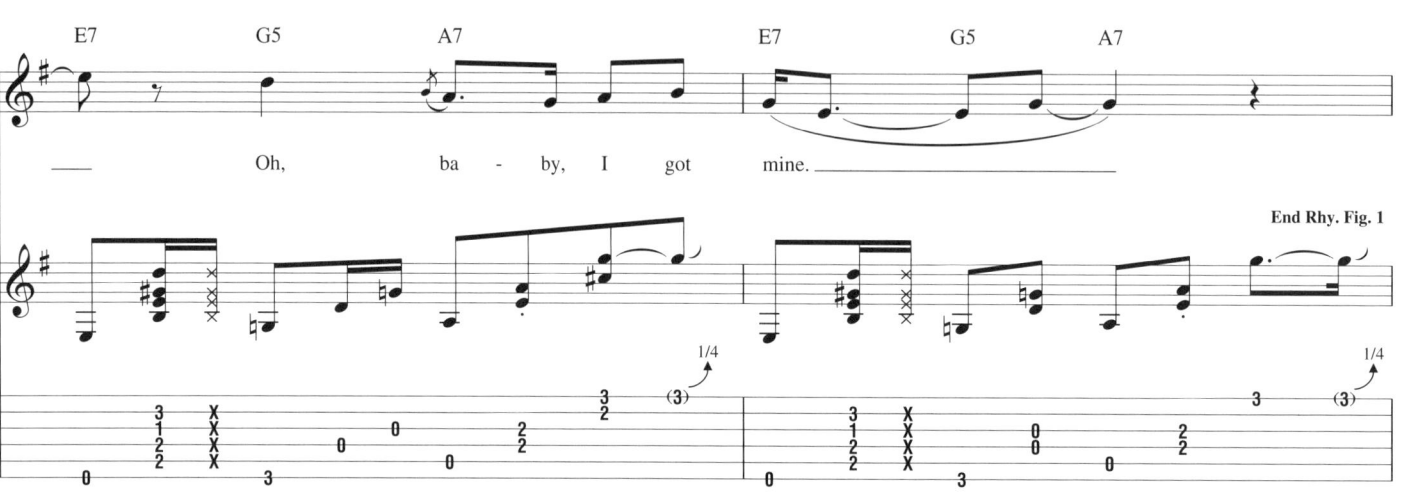

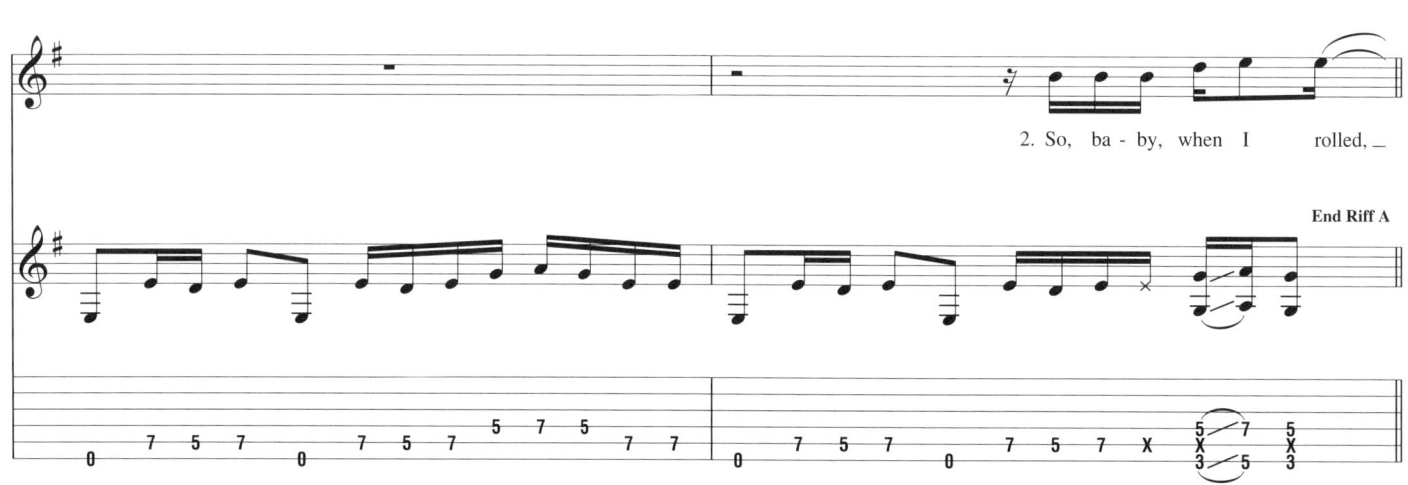

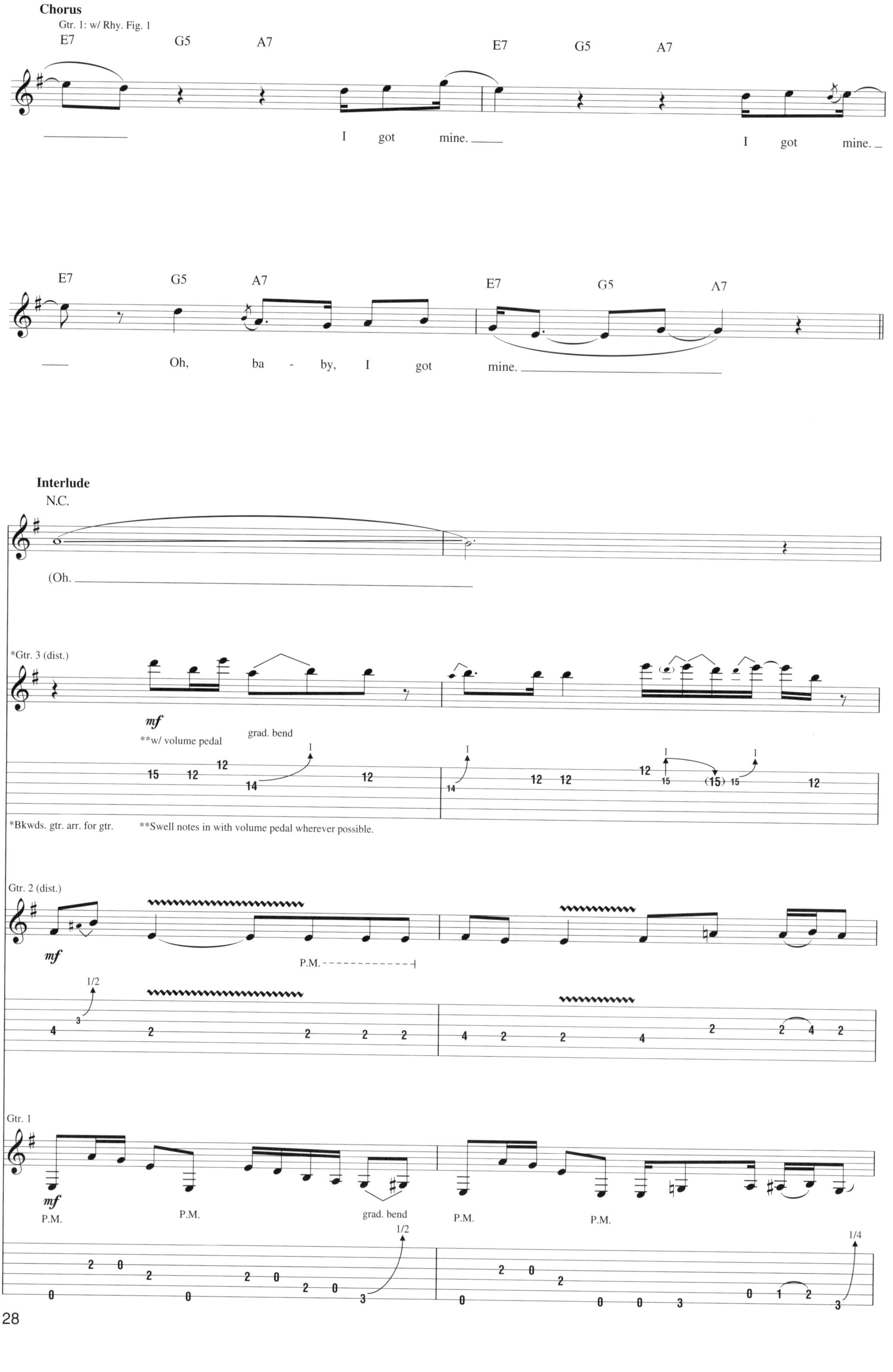

Chorus

Gtr. 1: w/ Rhy. Fig. 1

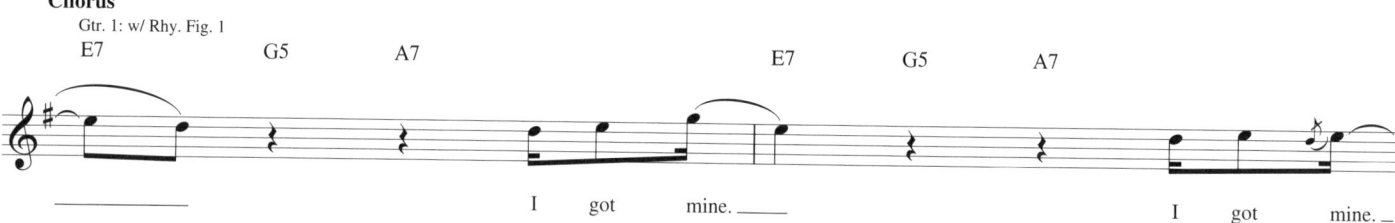

I got mine. ____ I got mine. ___

— Oh, ba - by, I got mine. _____

Interlude

N.C.

(Oh. _____

*Gtr. 3 (dist.)

mf

**w/ volume pedal   grad. bend

*Bkwds. gtr. arr. for gtr.   **Swell notes in with volume pedal wherever possible.

Gtr. 2 (dist.)

mf

P.M. - - - - - - - - - - - - |

Gtr. 1

mf

P.M.   P.M.   grad. bend   P.M.   P.M.

*Chord symbols reflect implied harmony (this meas.).

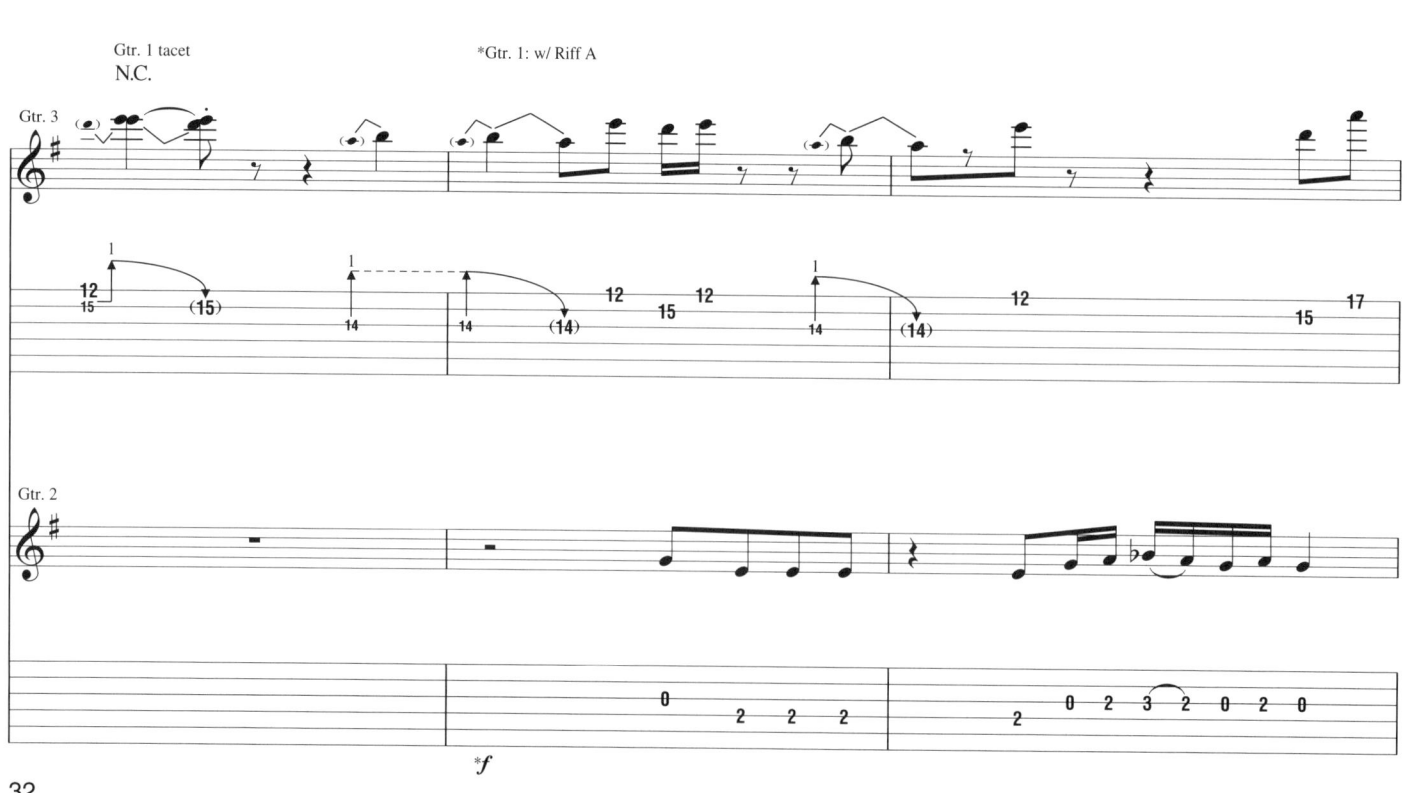

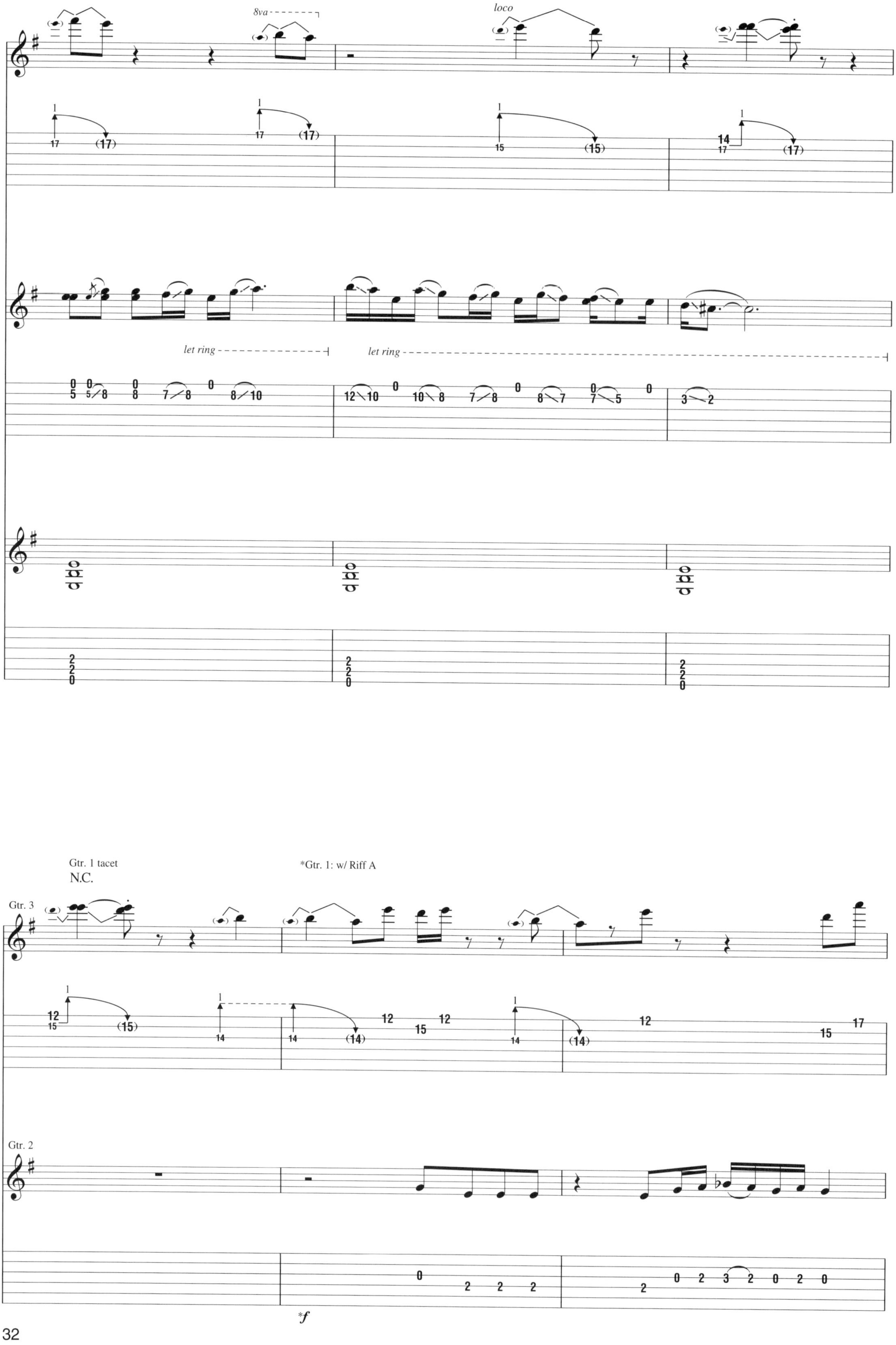
8va
loco
let ring
let ring
Gtr. 1 tacet
N.C.
*Gtr. 1: w/ Riff A
Gtr. 3
Gtr. 2
*f

Woh, I got mine. ___

let ring ----------

Chorus

Gtr. 1: w/ Rhy. Fig. 1

E7   G5   A7   E7   G5   A7

___   I got mine. _____   I got mine. ___

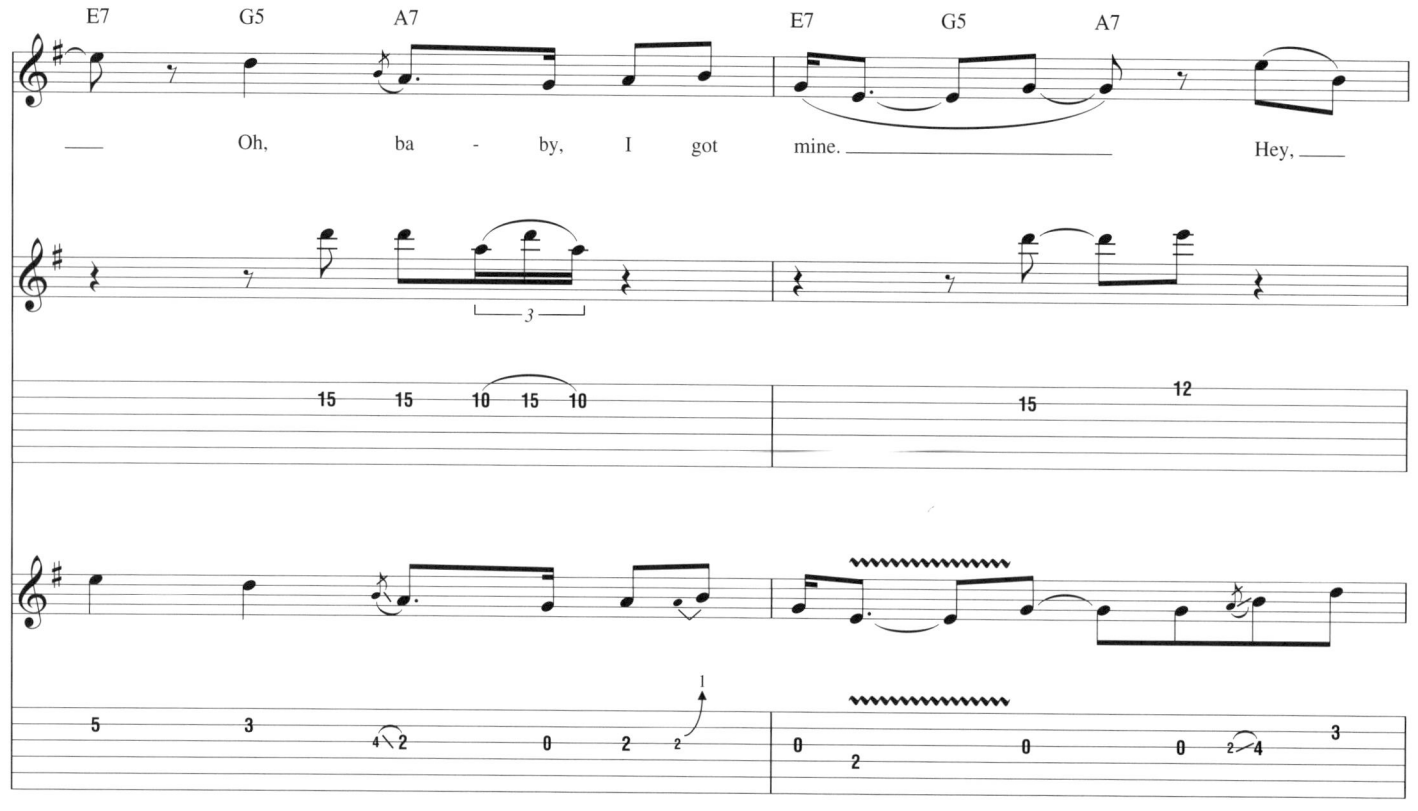

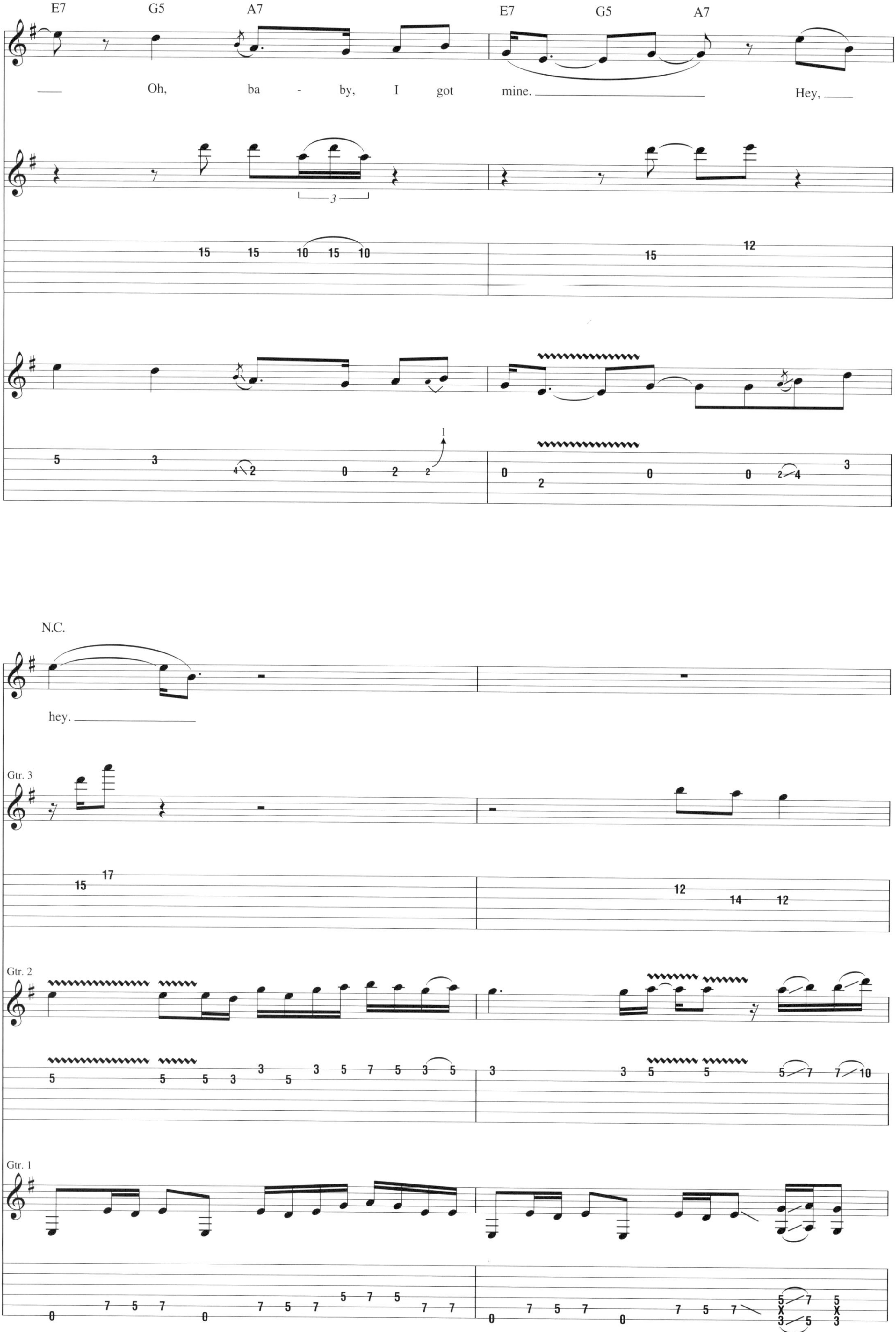
E7 G5 A7 E7 G5 A7
Oh, ba - by, I got mine. Hey,
N.C.
hey.
Gtr. 3
Gtr. 2
Gtr. 1

Outro
Tempo I

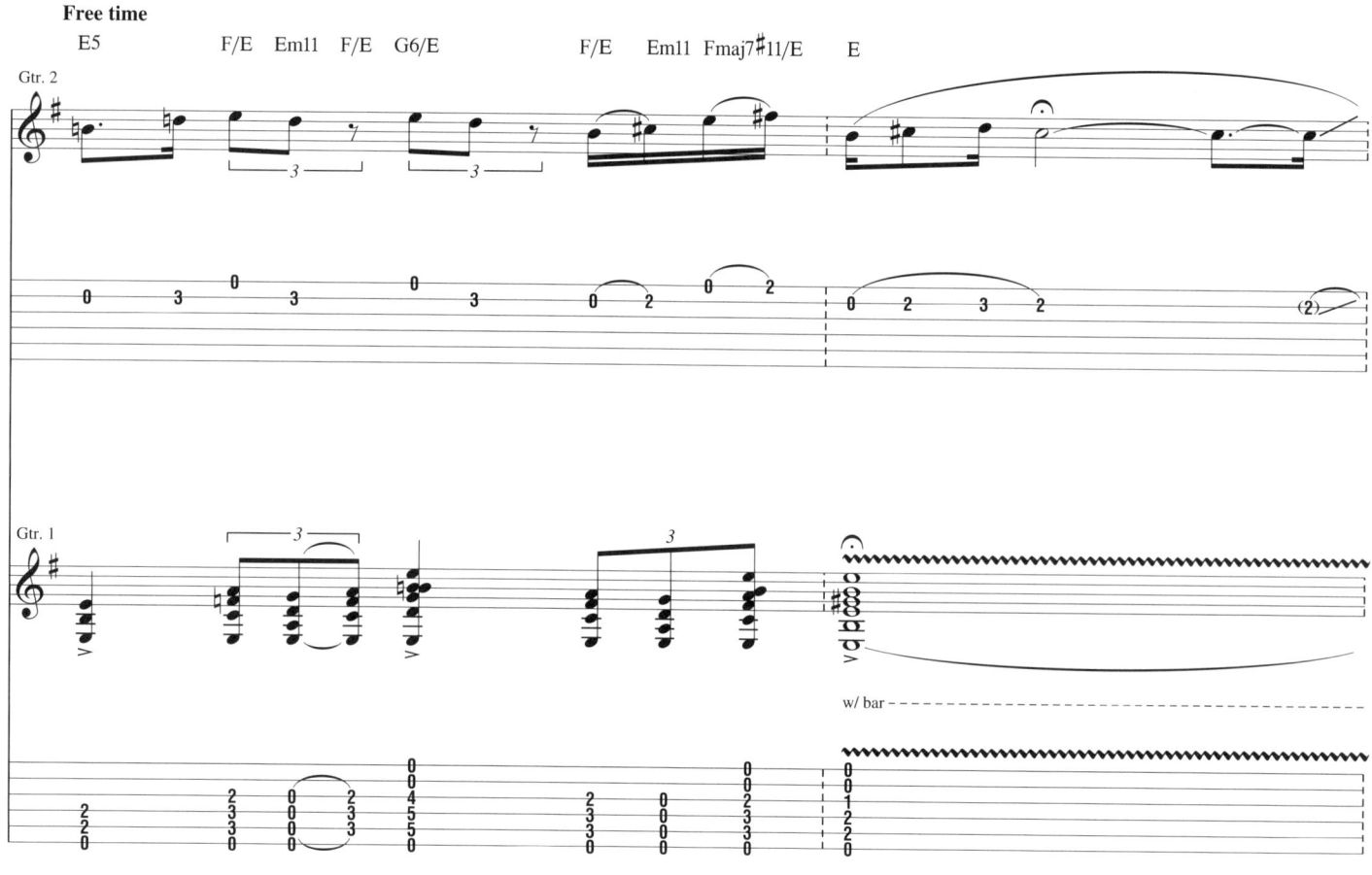

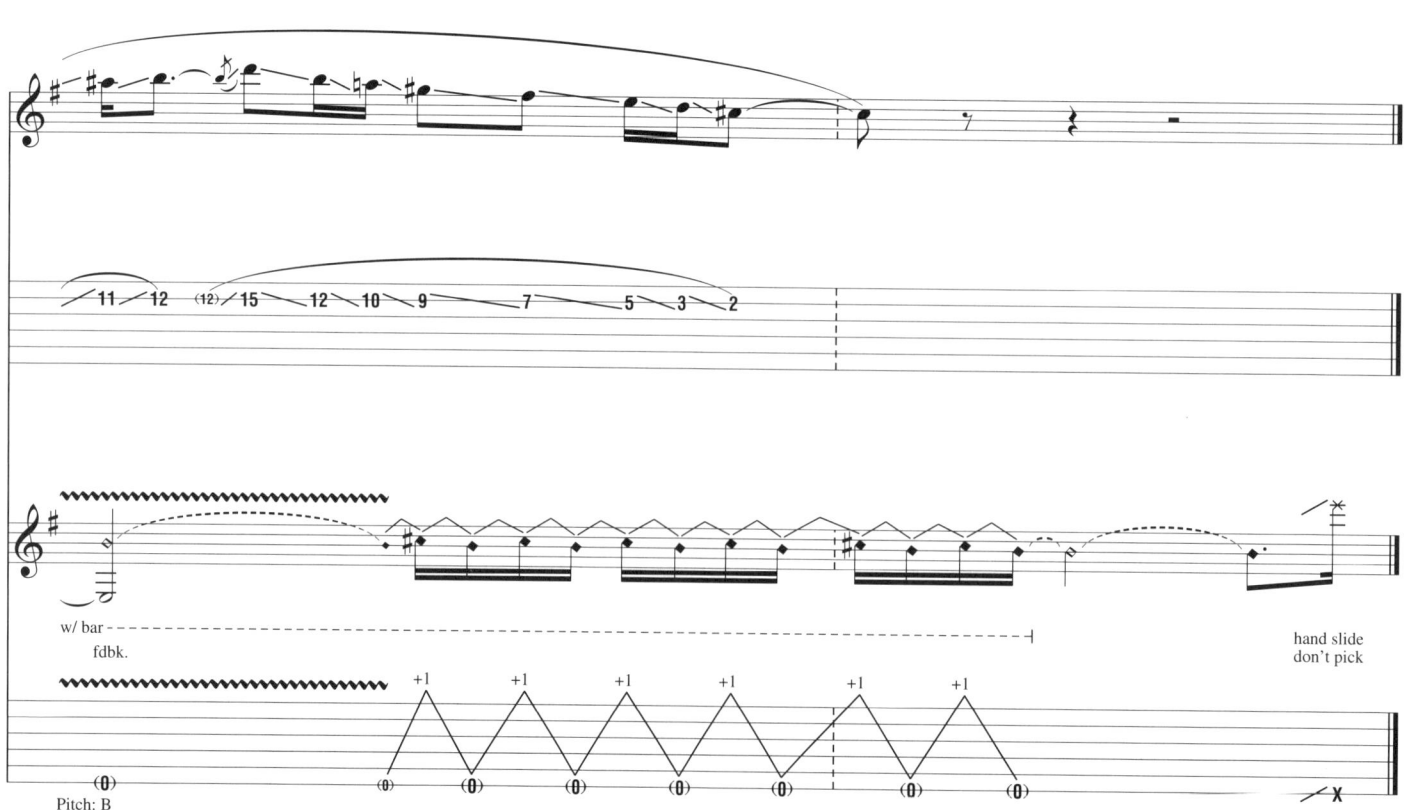

36

JUST GOT TO BE

Words and Music by
Dan Auerbach and Patrick Carney

Tune up 1 step:
(low to high:) F#-B-E-A-C#-F#

Intro
Moderate Rock ♩ = 88

N.C.

Gtr. 1 (dist.)

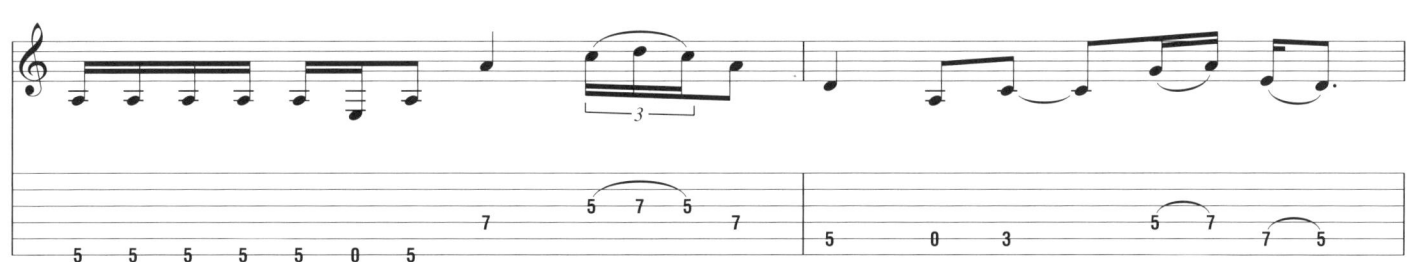

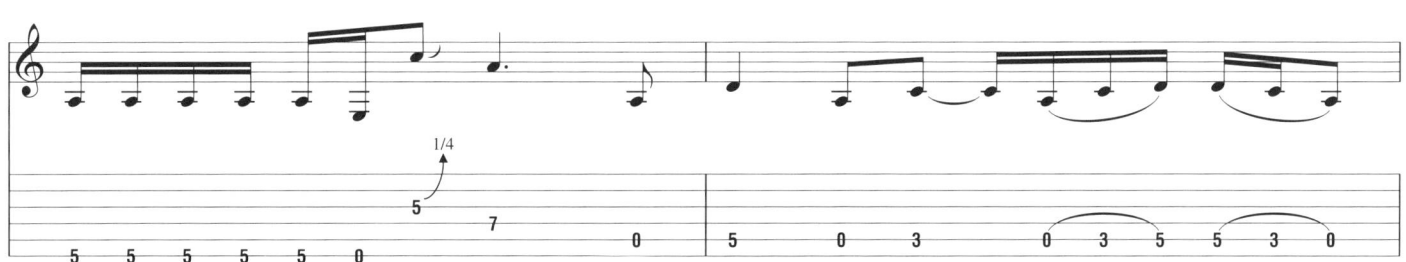

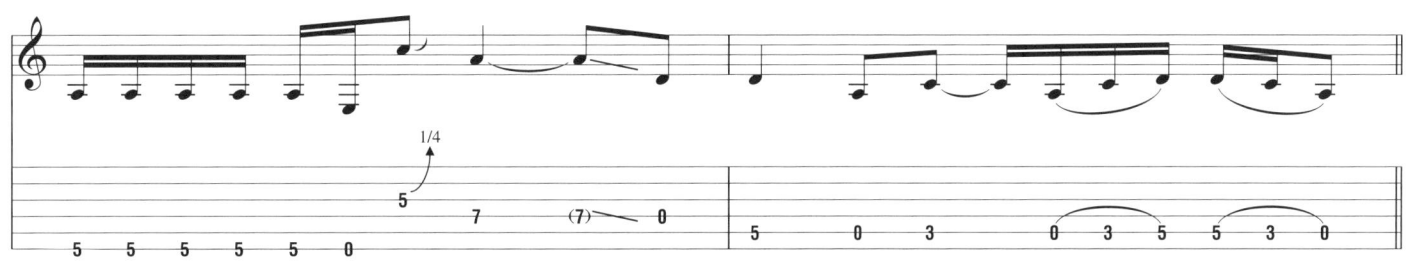

37

Verse

1. When it comes to pride ___
2. Ev - il hearts

2nd time, Gtr. 1: w/ Fill 1

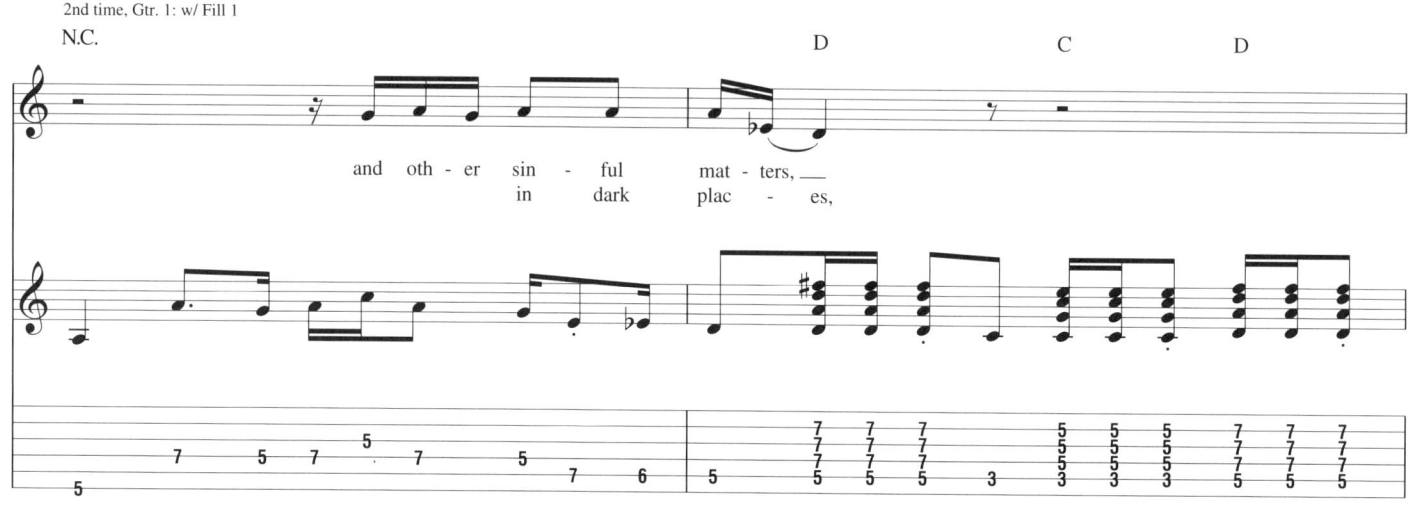

and oth - er sin - ful mat - ters, ___
in dark plac - es,

you're gon - na be mis - led, ___
but now I find ___ it

Fill 1
Gtr. 1

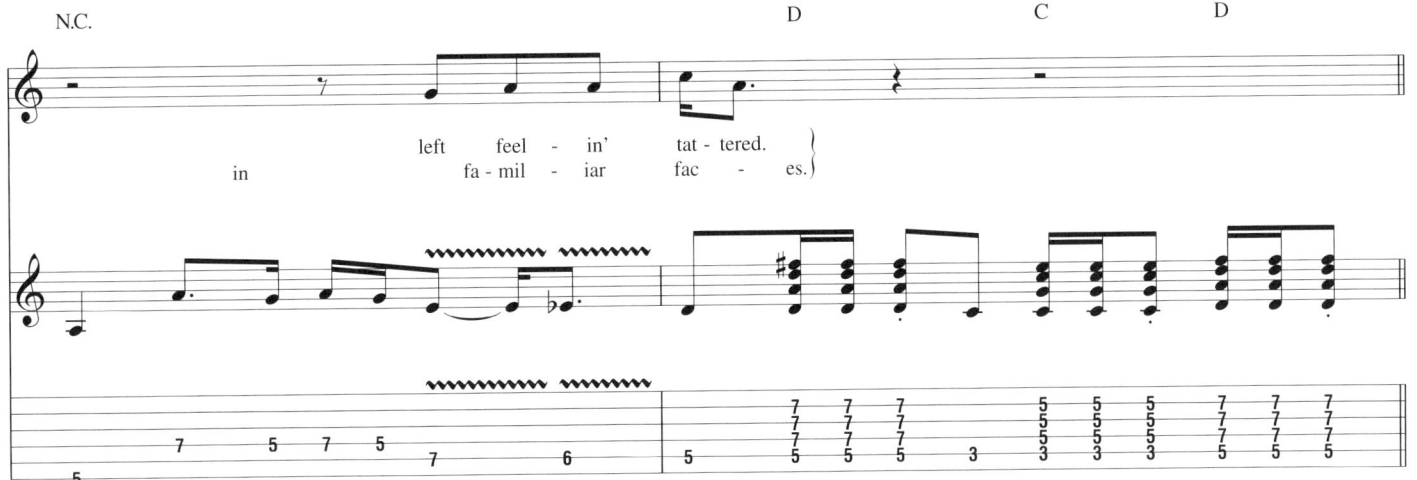

Pre-Chorus

Chorus

1st time, Gtr. 1: w/ Riff A (2 times)
2nd time, Gtr. 1: w/ Riff A
N.C.

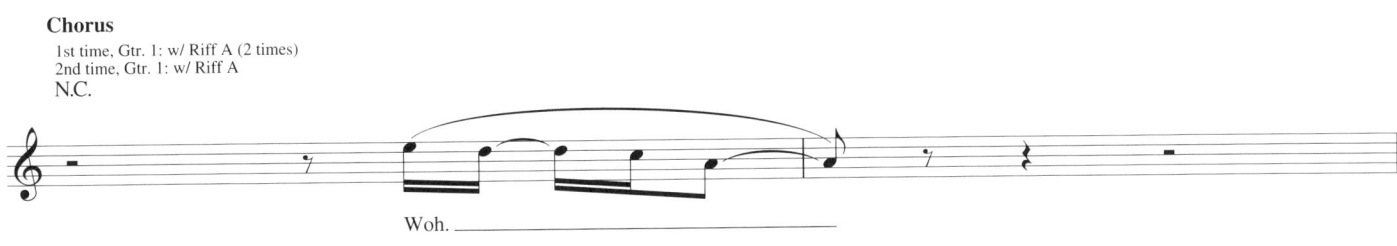

2nd time, Gtr. 1: w/ Fill 2

Yeah.

2nd time, Gtr. 1: w/ Riff A

You just got to be ____

Gtr. 1

Gtr. 1: w/ Riff A

the best thing for me. ____

Interlude

N.C.

Gtr. 1

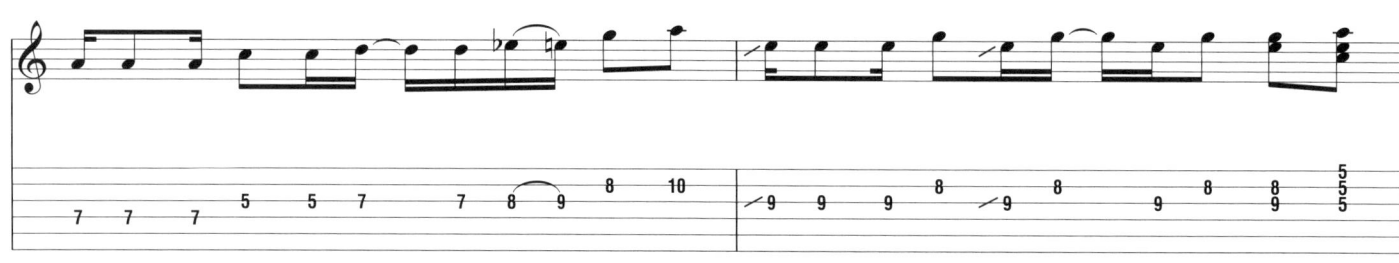

Fill 2

Gtr. 1

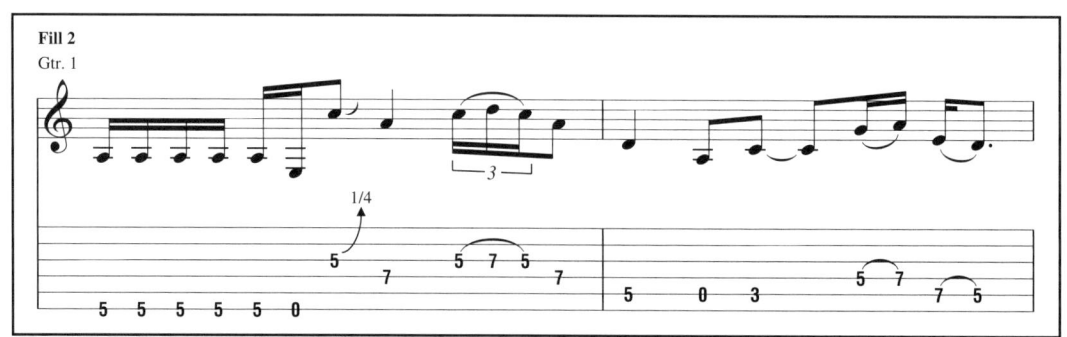

Outro

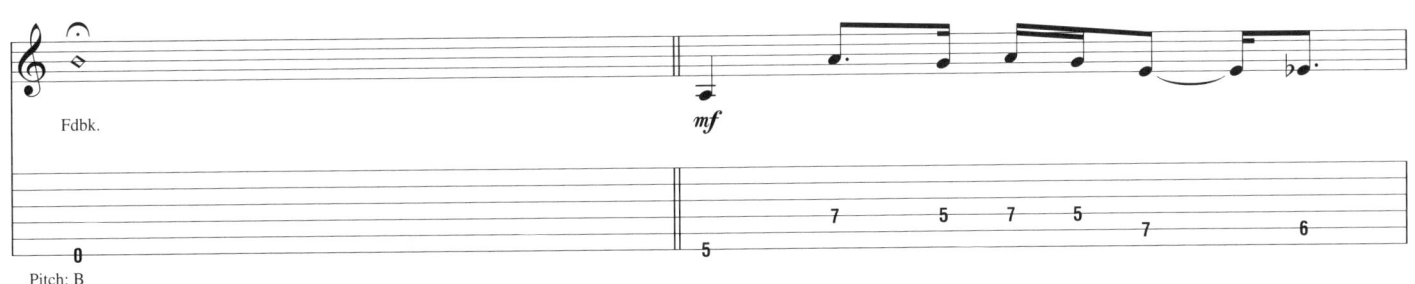

Fdbk.

Pitch: B

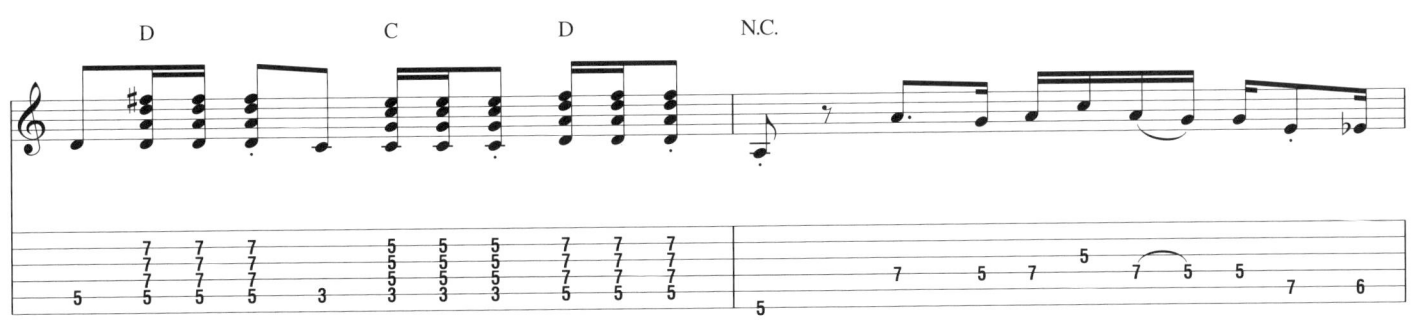

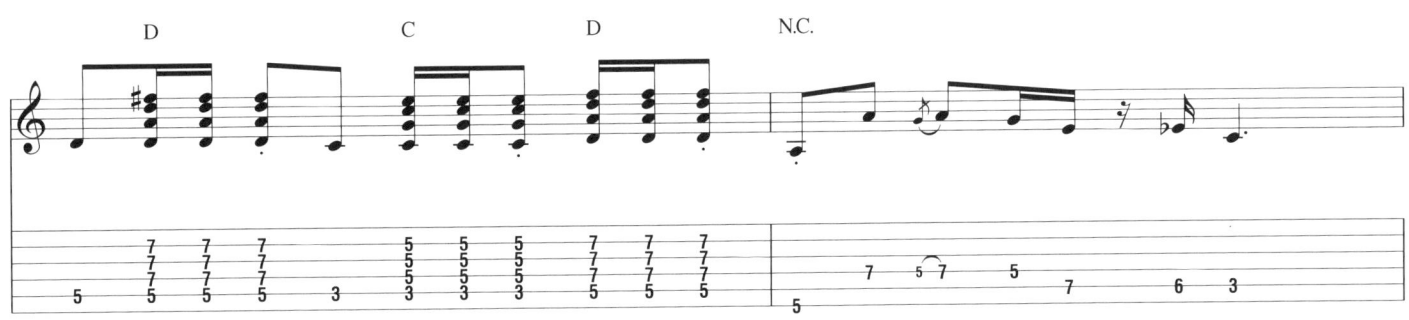

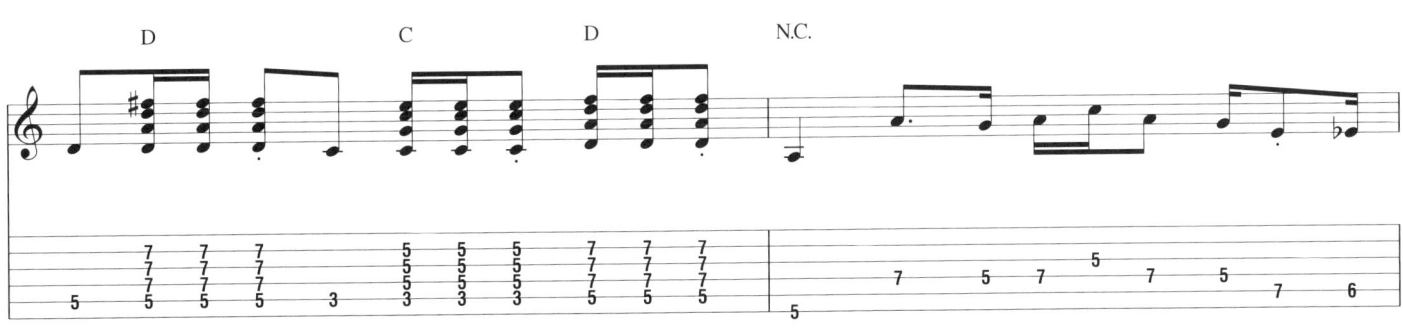

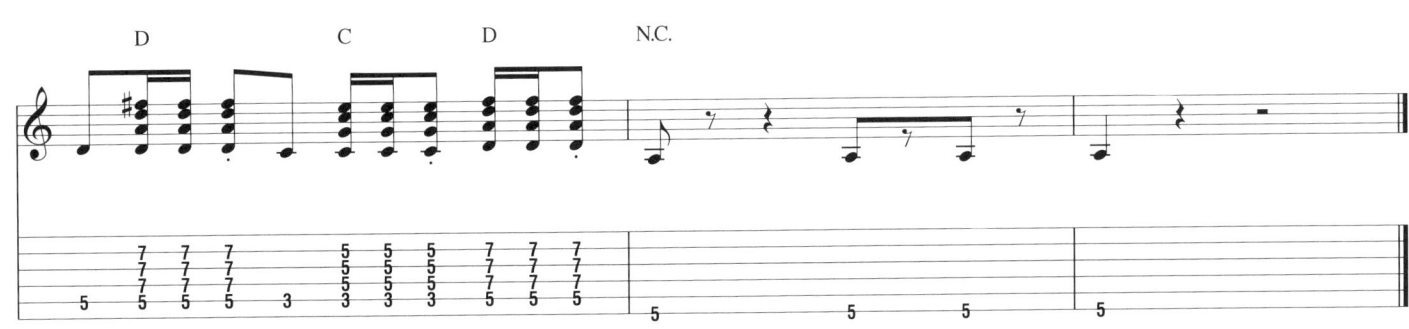

PSYCHOTIC GIRL

Words and Music by
Dan Auerbach and Patrick Carney

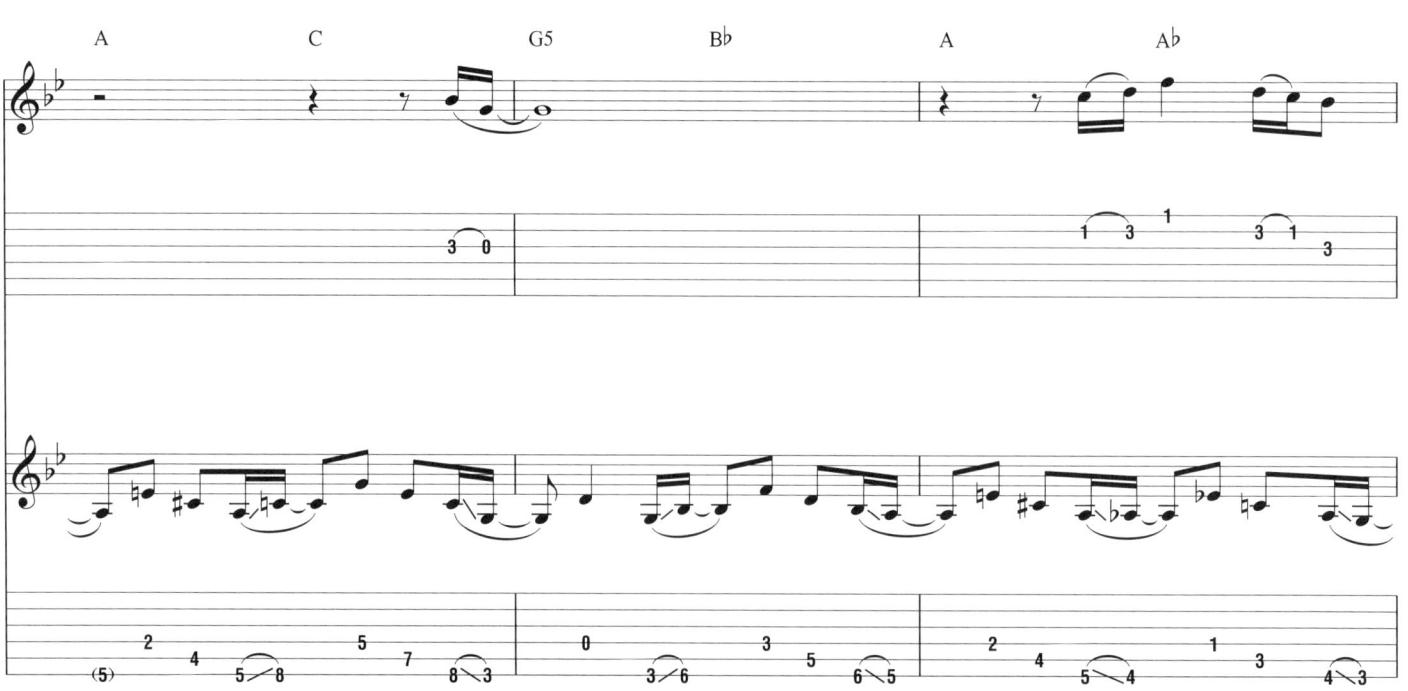

Verse

Gtr. 2: w/ Riff A (3 times)

heard   you threw   your man a - round,

Gtr. 1

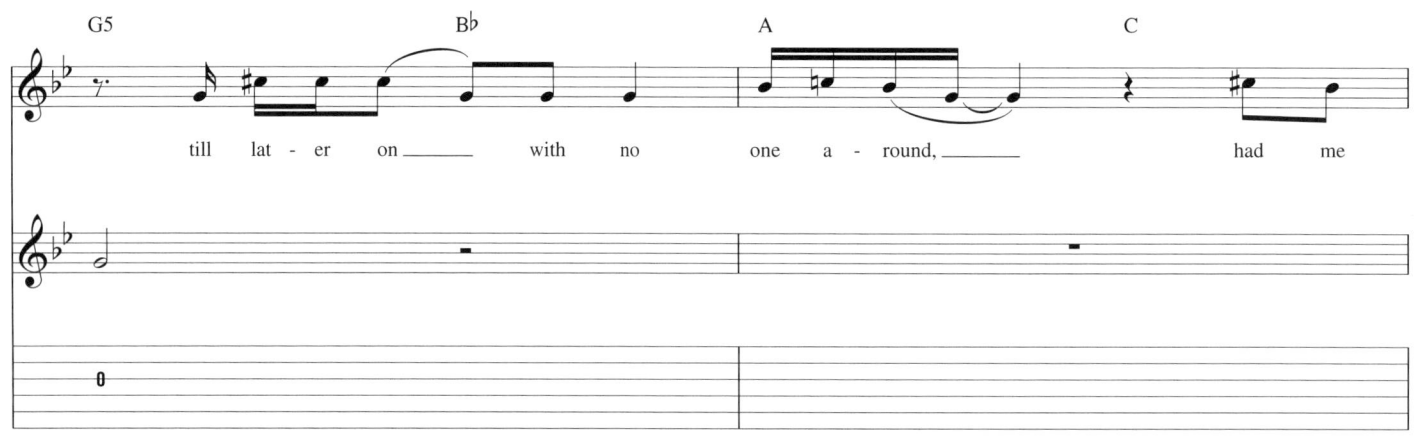

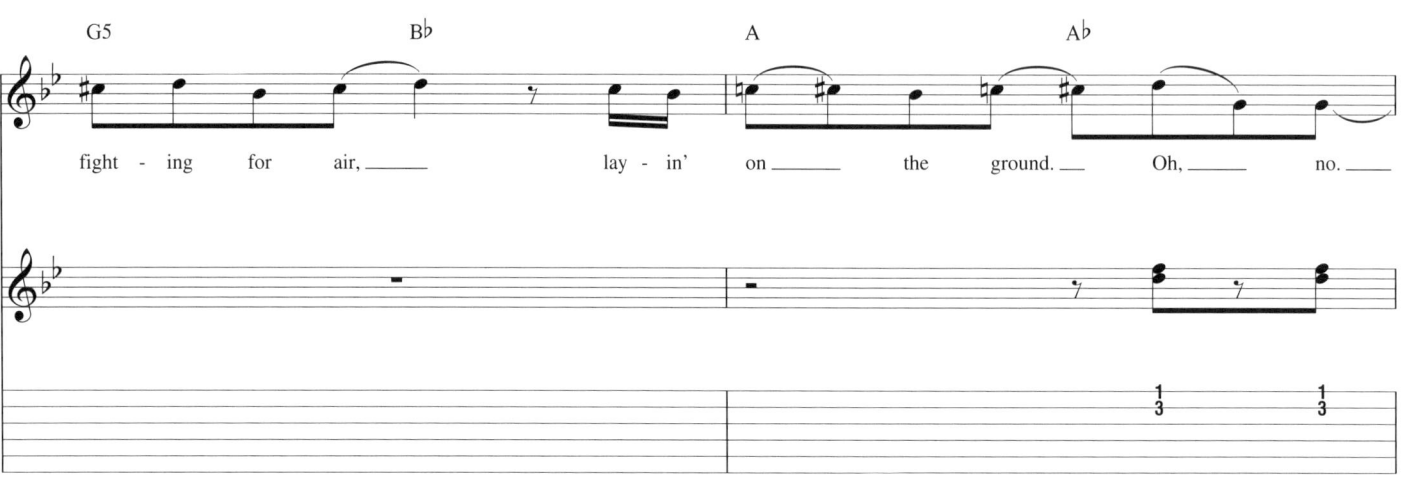

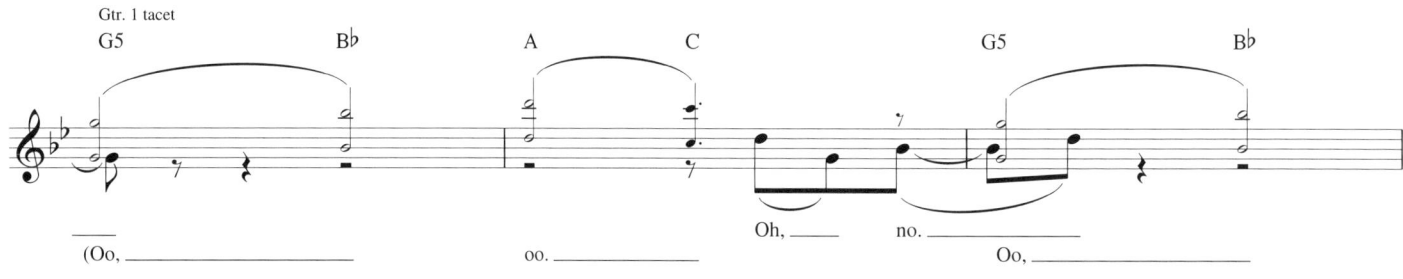

Chorus

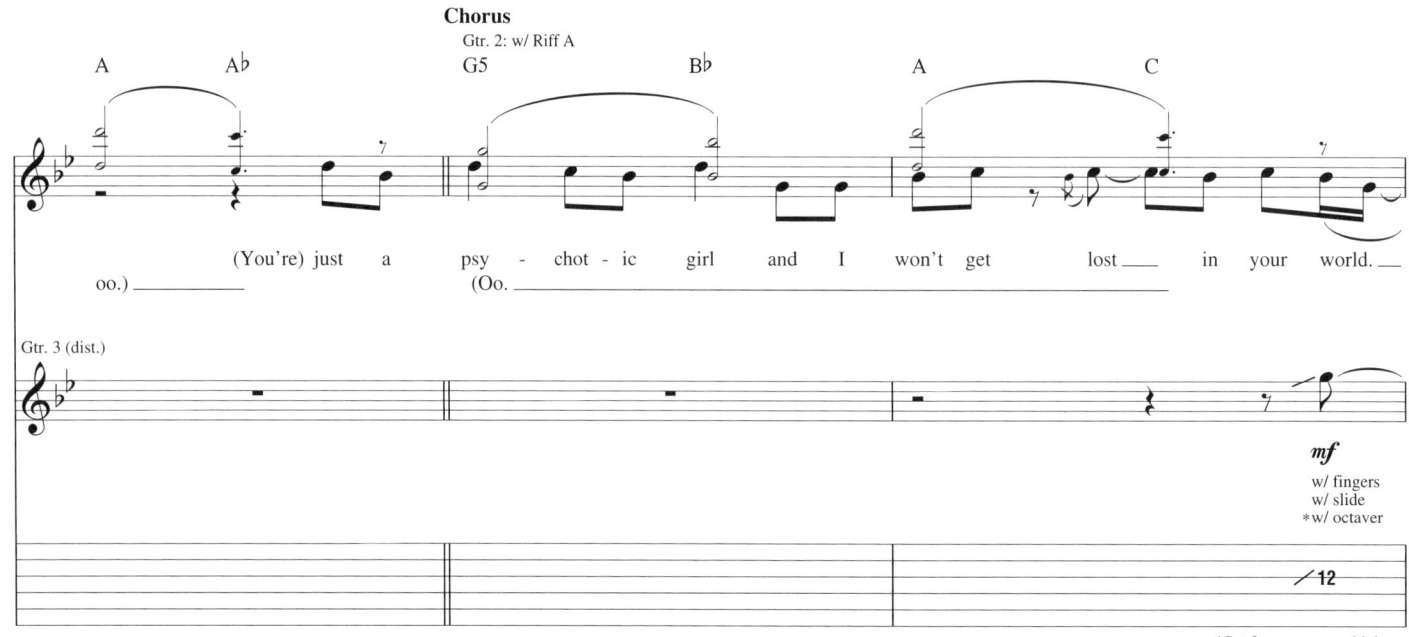

*Set for one octave higher.

46

Interlude

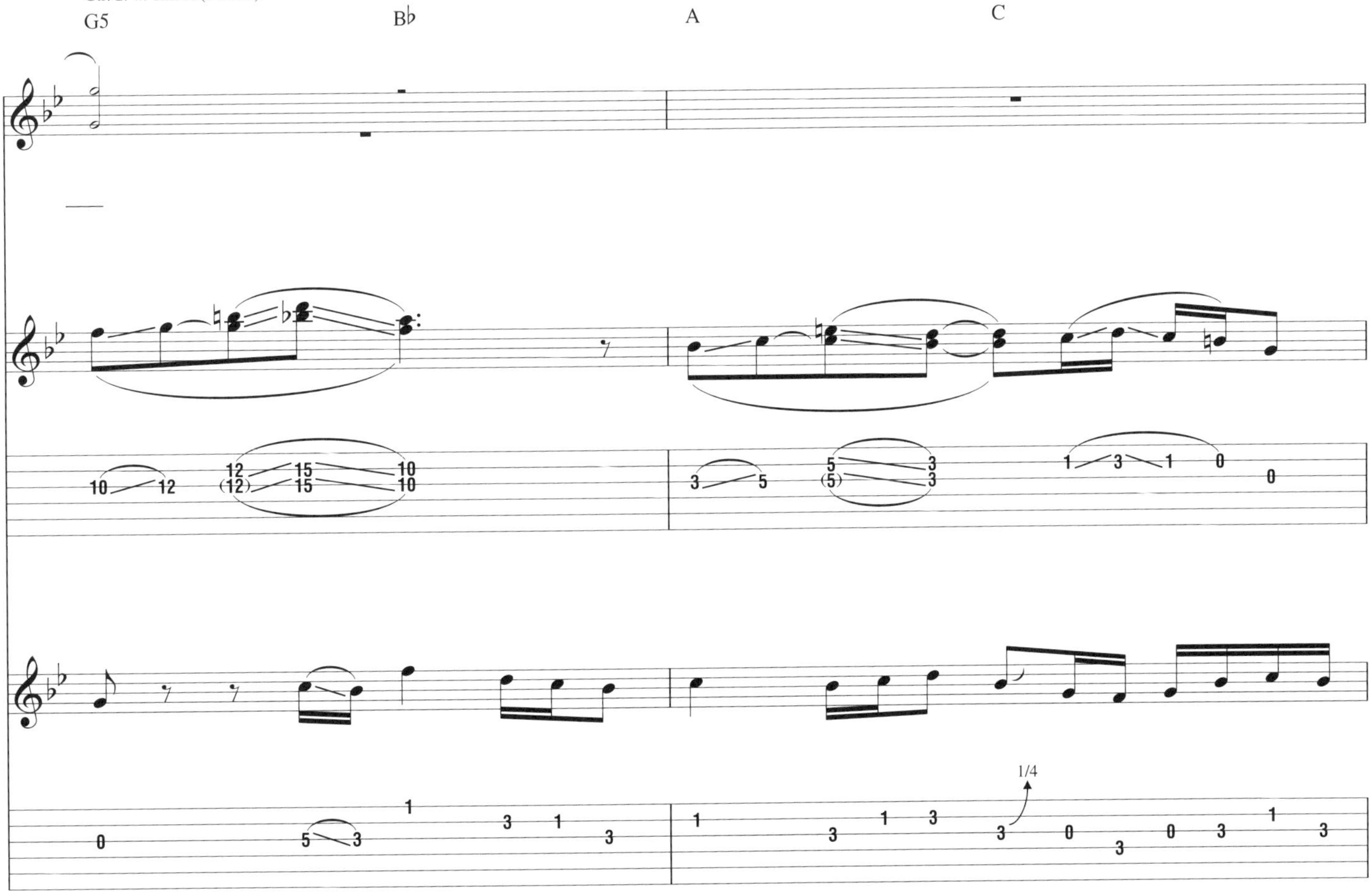

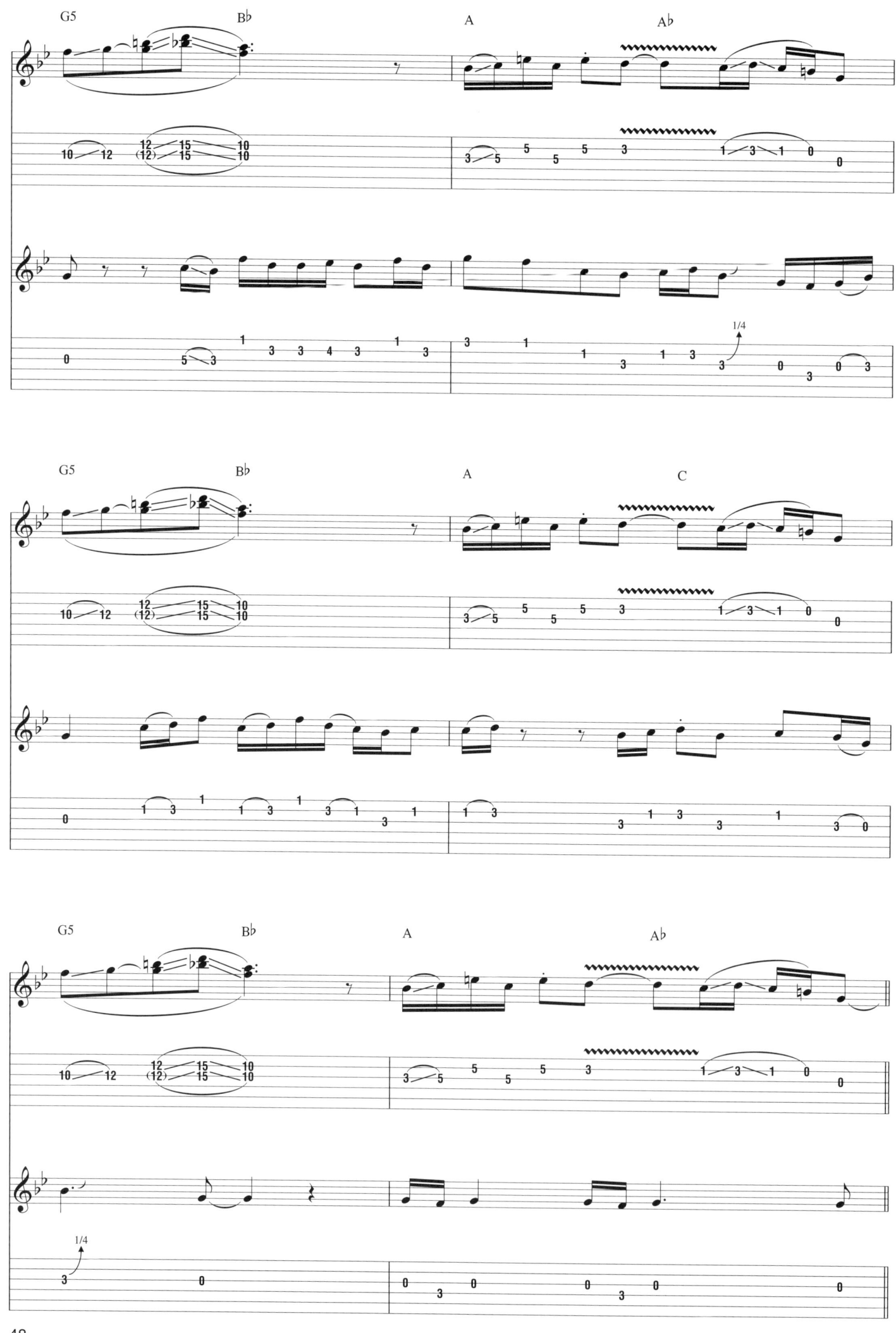

49

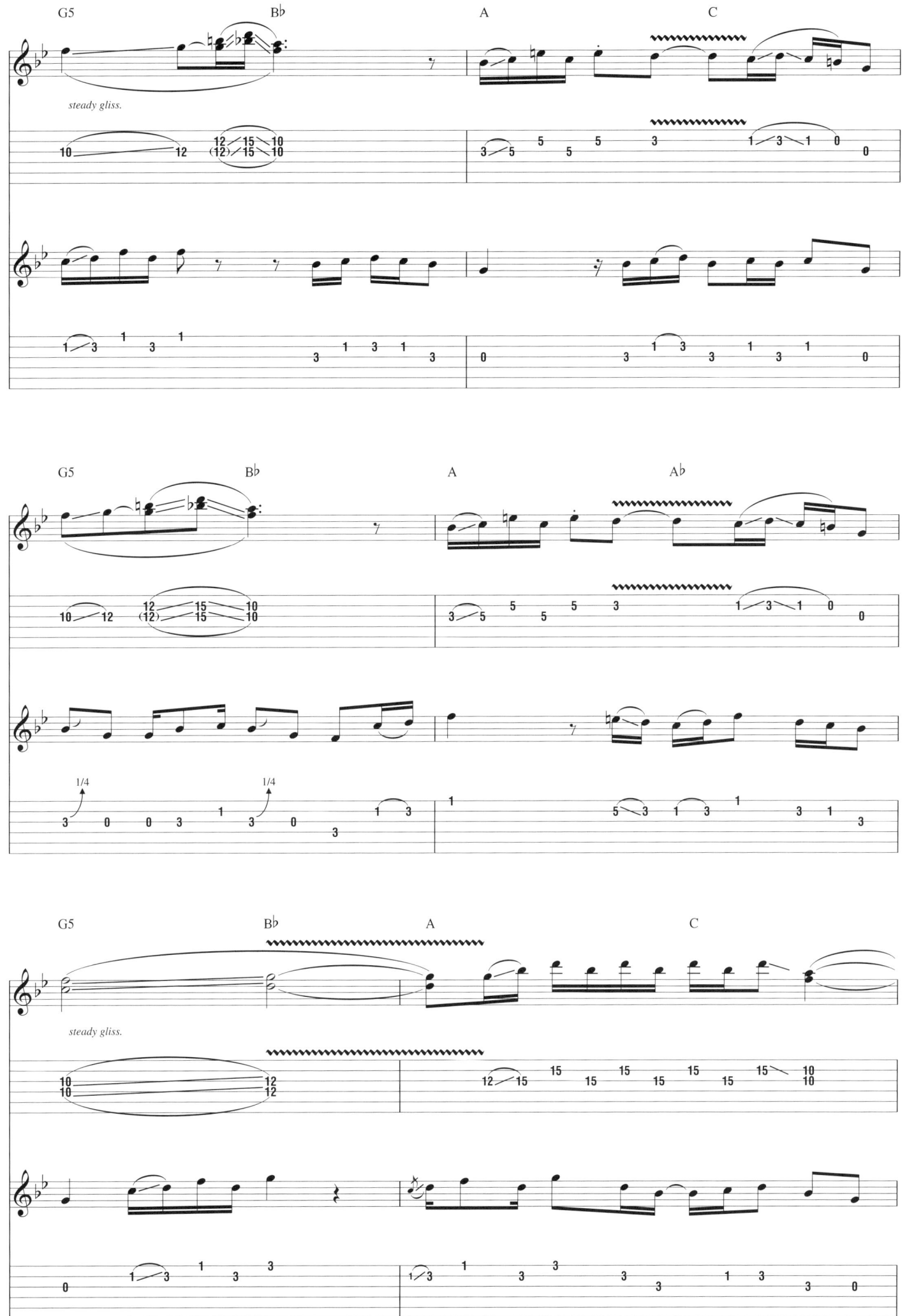

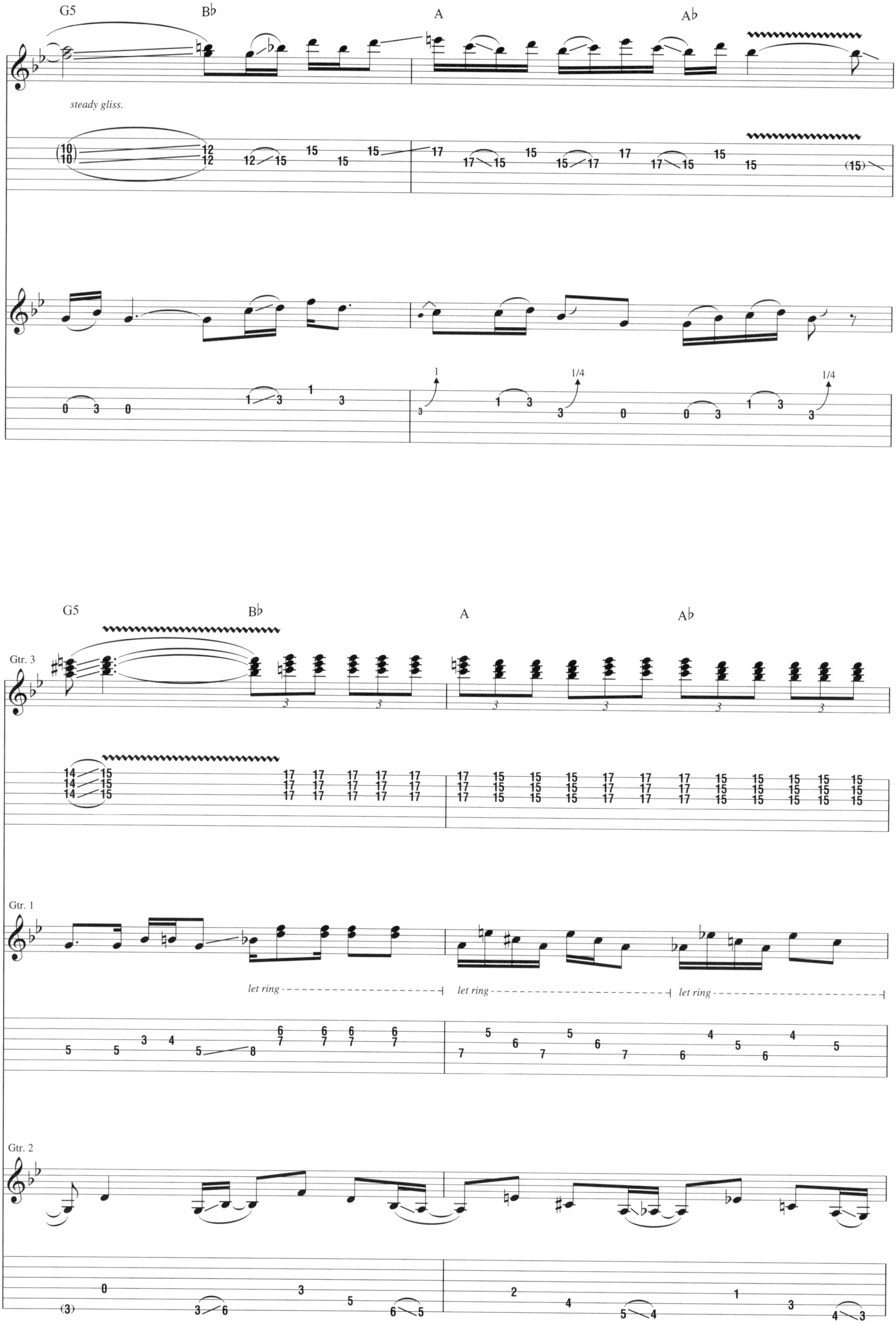
G5
B♭
A
A♭
steady gliss.
G5
B♭
A
A♭
Gtr. 3
Gtr. 1
let ring
let ring
let ring
Gtr. 2

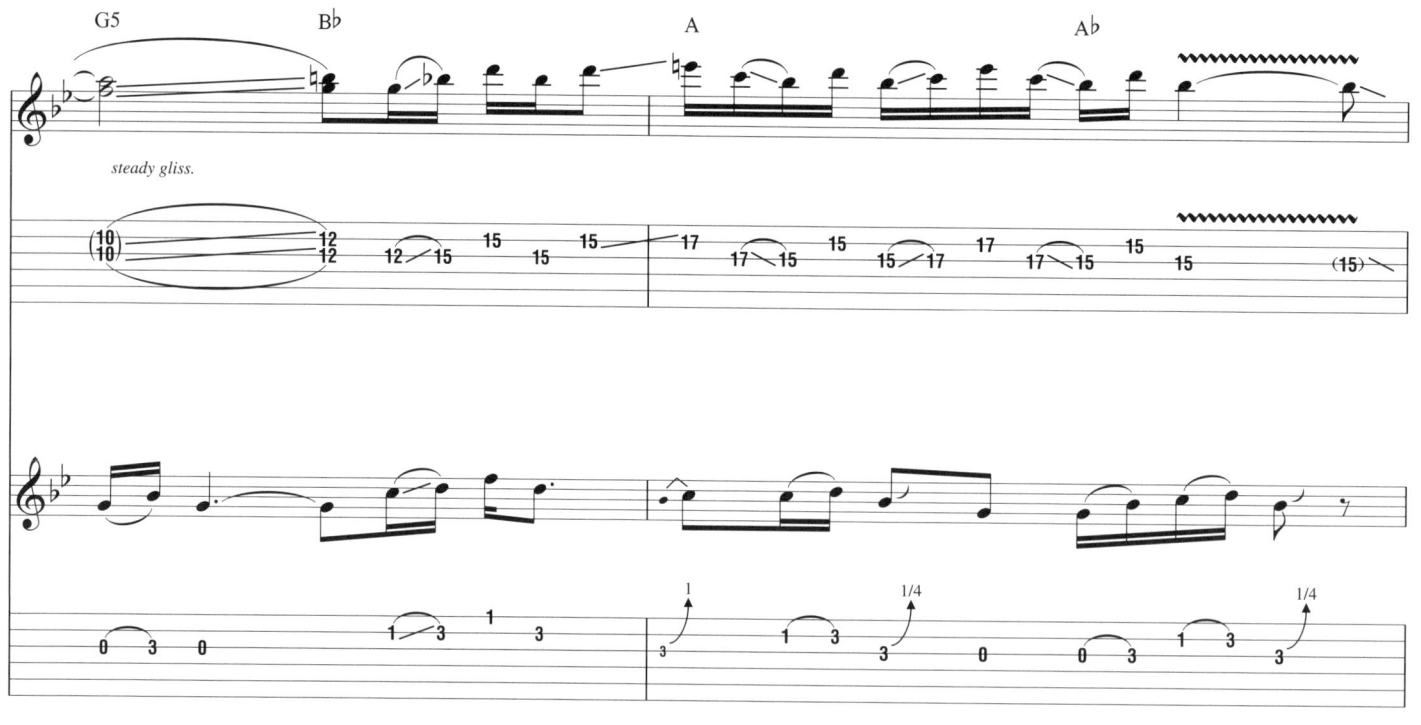

Gtr. 2 tacet
G5
steady gliss.
1/4
*Gtr. 4
mp
*Banjo arr. for gtr.
Gtr. 3 tacet
Gtr. 1
Gtr. 4

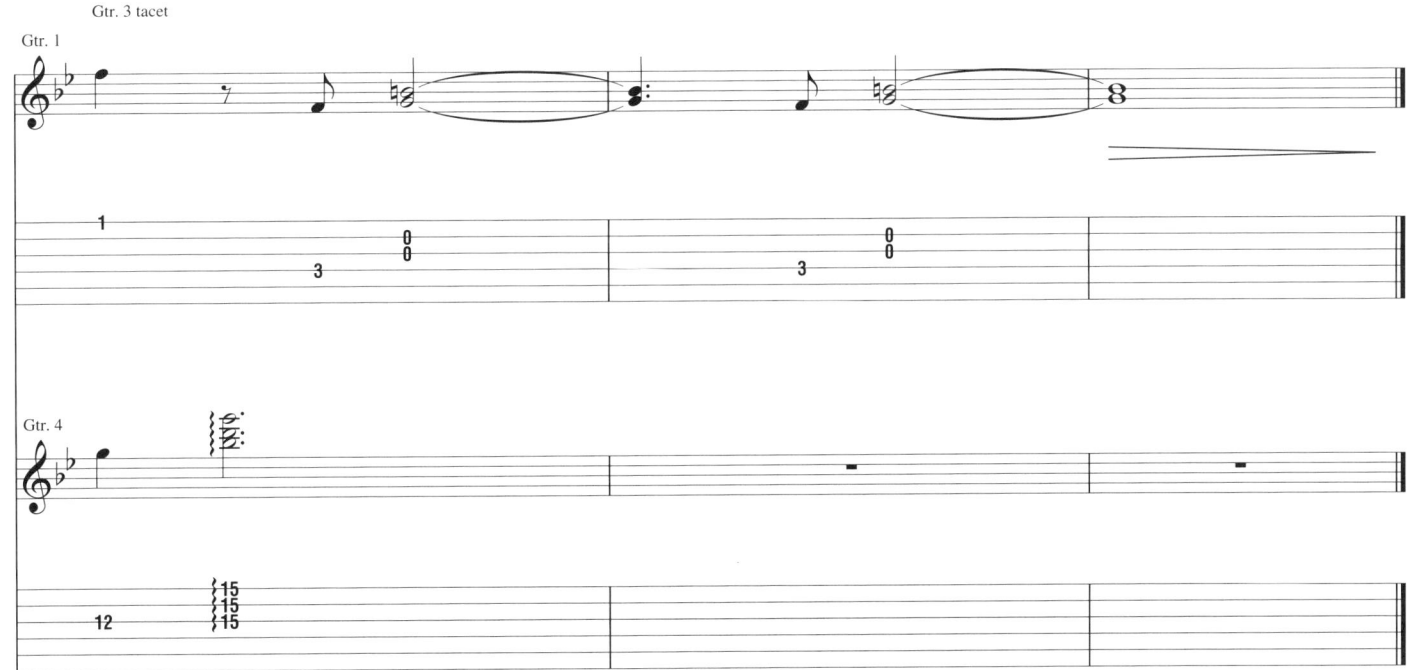

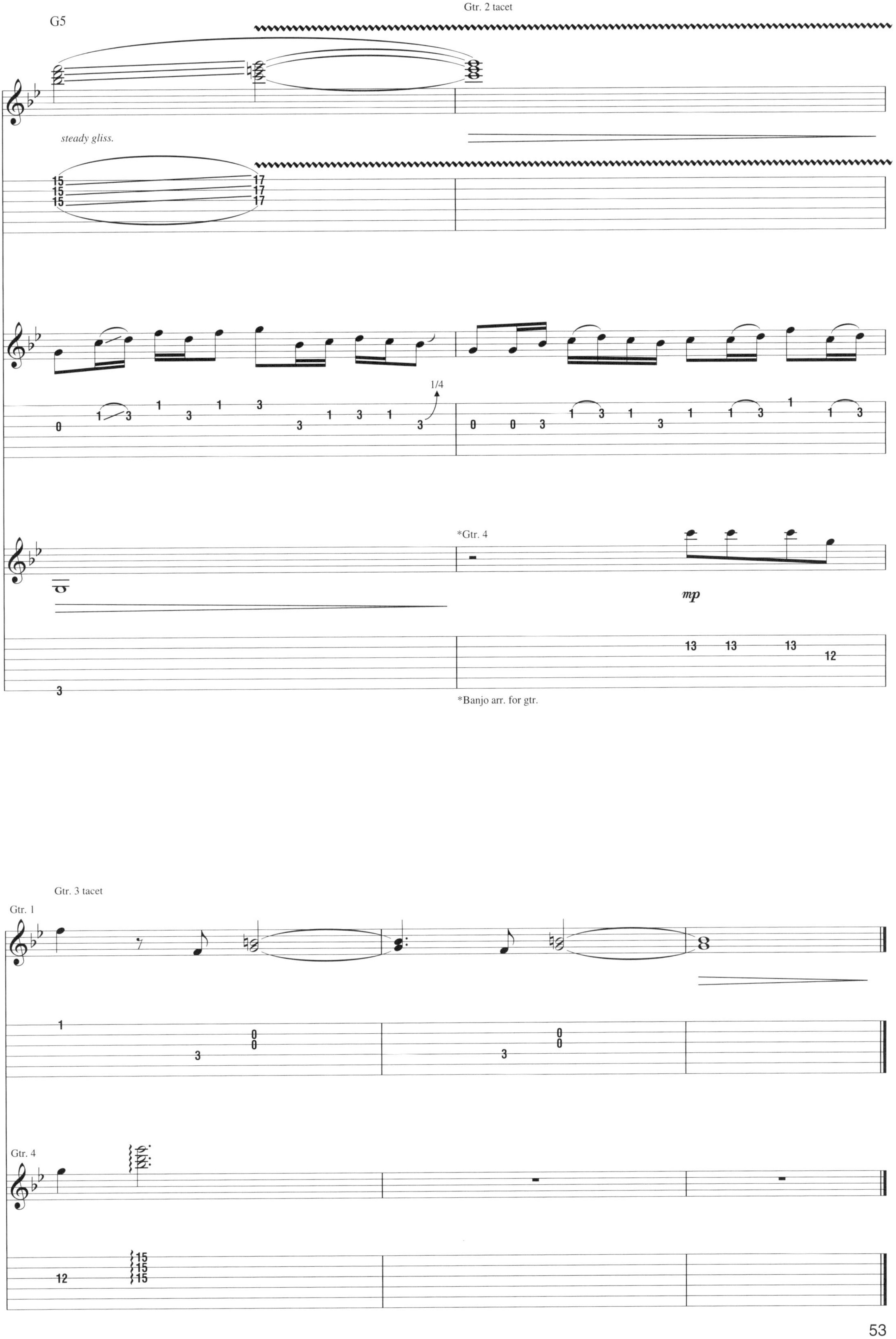

SET YOU FREE

Words and Music by
Dan Auerbach and Patrick Carney

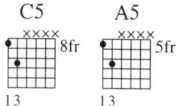

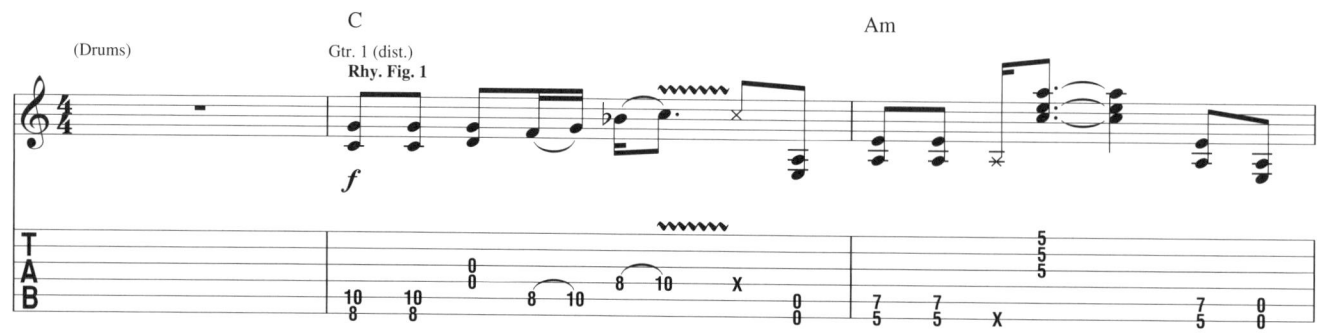

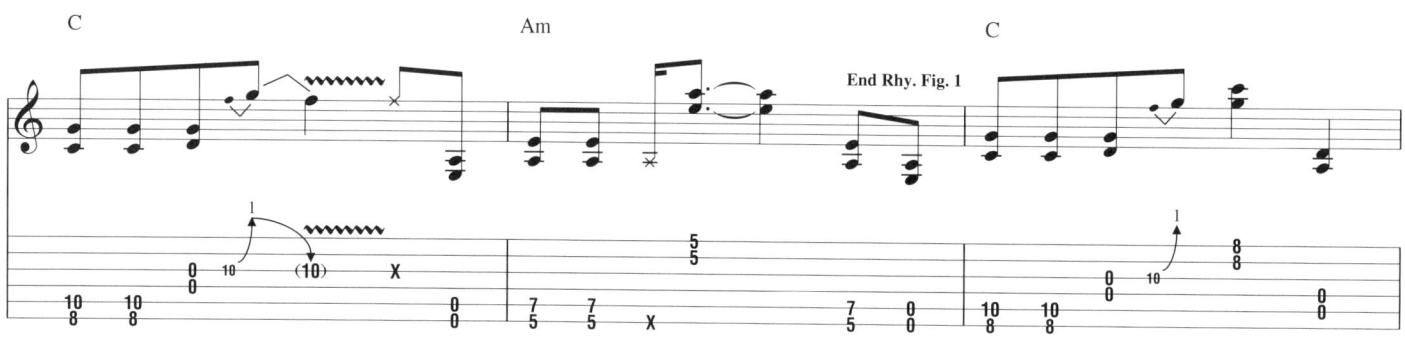

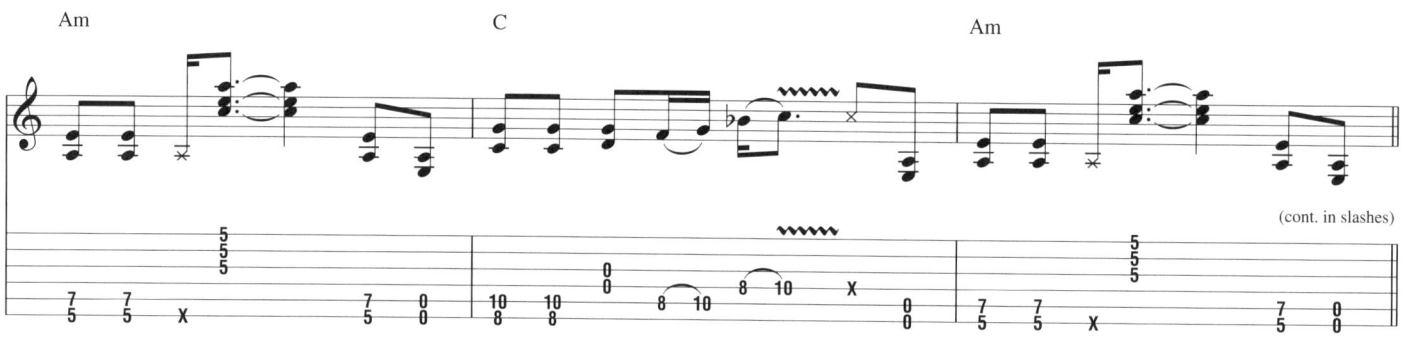

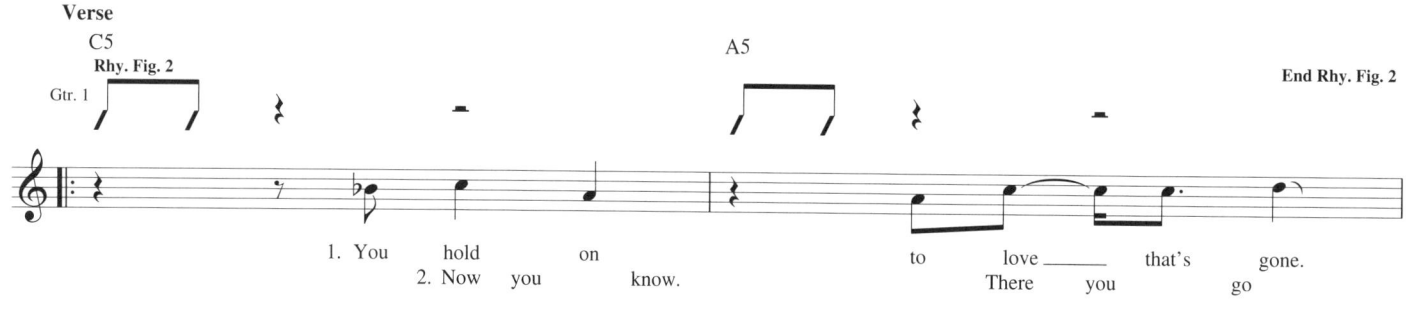

Guitar Solo

Gtr. 1: w/ Rhy. Fig. 2 (4 times)

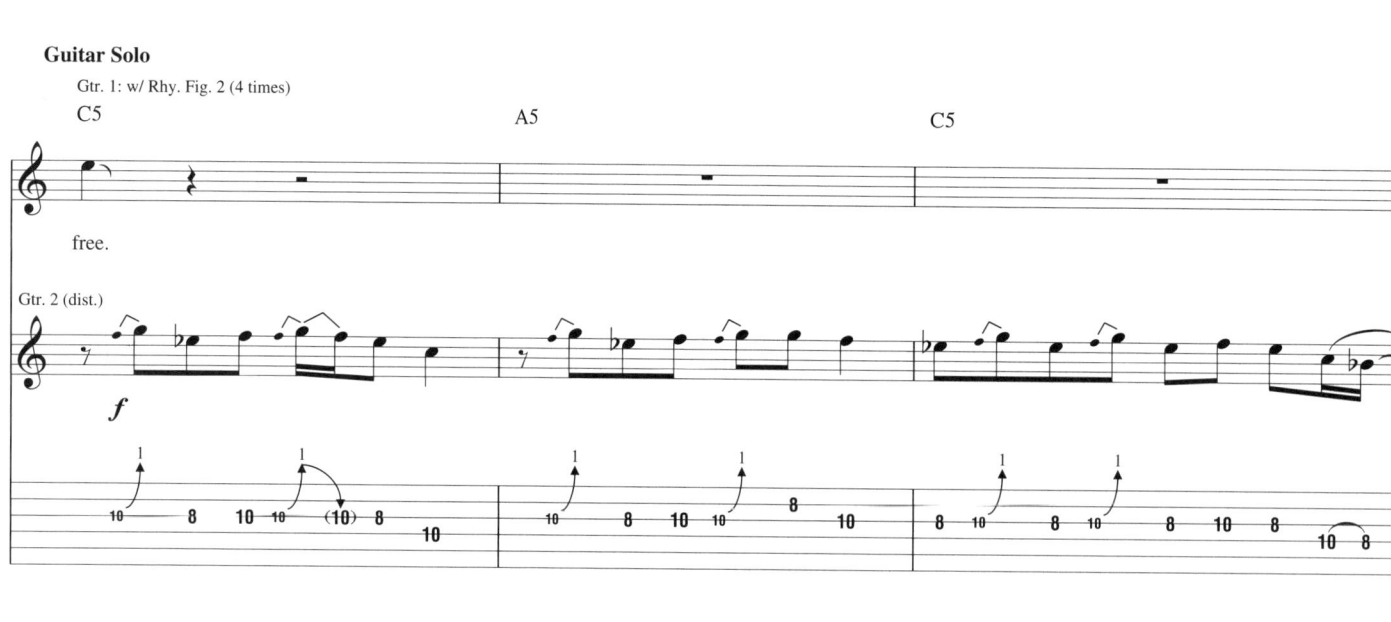

free.

Gtr. 2 (dist.)

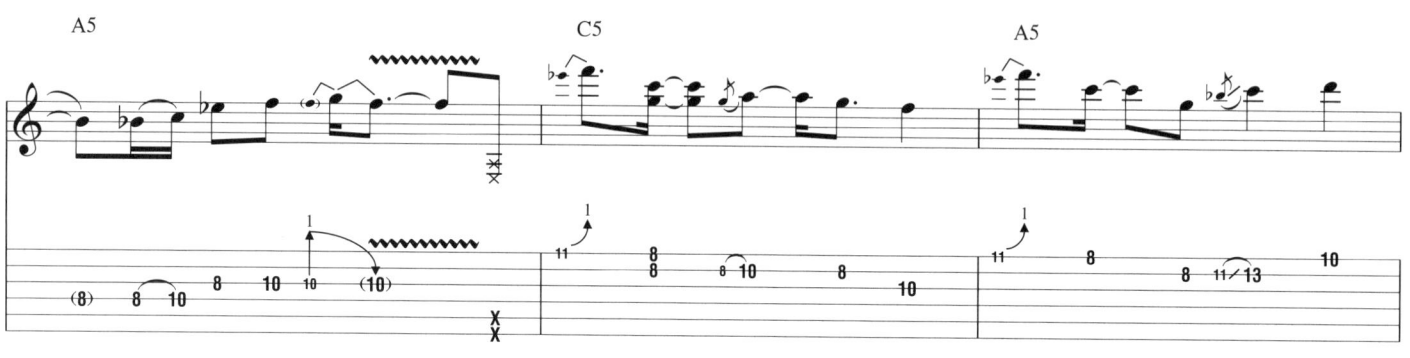

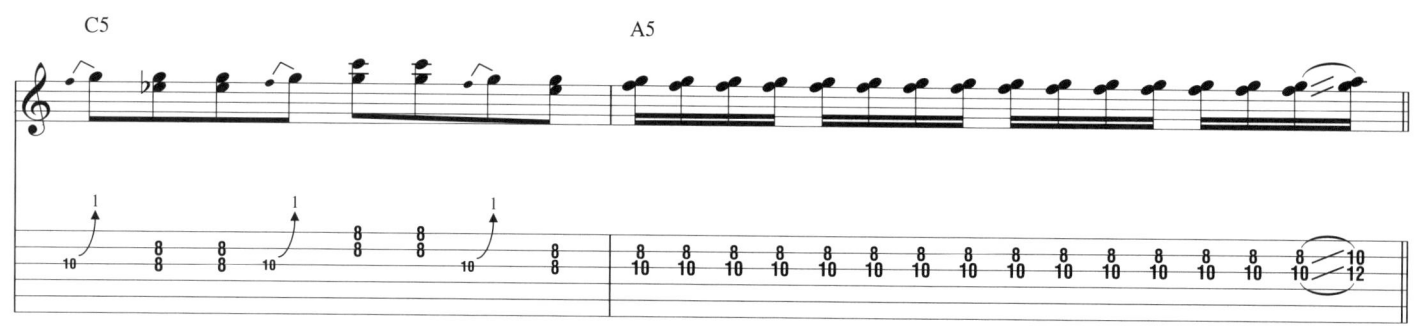

Verse

Gtr. 2 tacet

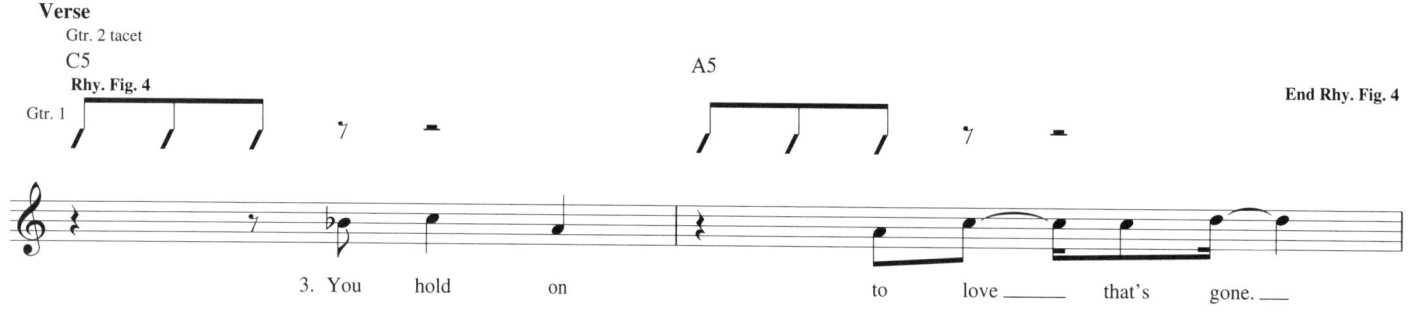

3. You hold on to love _____ that's gone. _____

Gtr. 1: w/ Rhy. Fig. 4 (3 times)

Run a mile to see him _____ smile. But you don't know _____

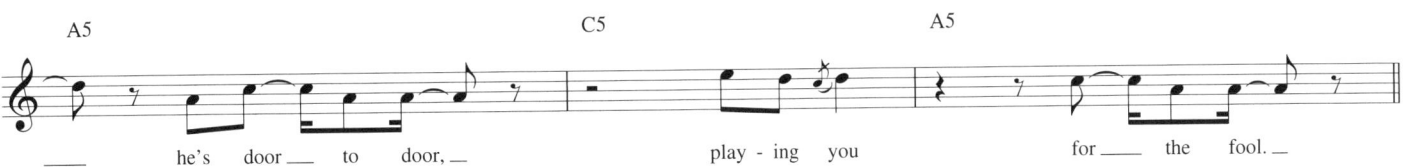

he's door __ to door, __ play - ing you for __ the fool. __

Chorus

Let him go. ___

Walk out the door __

mf

Gtr. 1: w/ Rhy. Fig. 3 (2 times)

and come to me. __

I'm gon - na set you

Outro

Gtr. 1

free. __

I'll set you free. __

I'll set you

free. __

I'll set you __ free.

I'll set you __ free.

I'll set you

free. ____

STRANGE TIMES

Words and Music by
Dan Auerbach and Patrick Carney

Calm - ing   rest - less   mobs, _____   eas - ing   all ___

____   of   their,   all   of   their ___   fear. _____   Strange ___

Gtr. 2 (dist.)   **Riff B**   **End Riff B**

mf

2

Chorus
Half-time feel

A#m   D#m   3   3

Gtr. 1

times ___   are   here. _____   Strange ___

Riff C

6   6   6   6   6   6   6   6   2   2   2   2   2   2   2   2

End half-time feel

A#m   D#m

(cont. in notation)

times ___   are   here. _____

End Riff C

6   6   6   6   6   6   6   6   2   2   2   2   2   2   2   2

59

THICKFREAKNESS

Words and Music by
Dan Auerbach and Patrick Carney

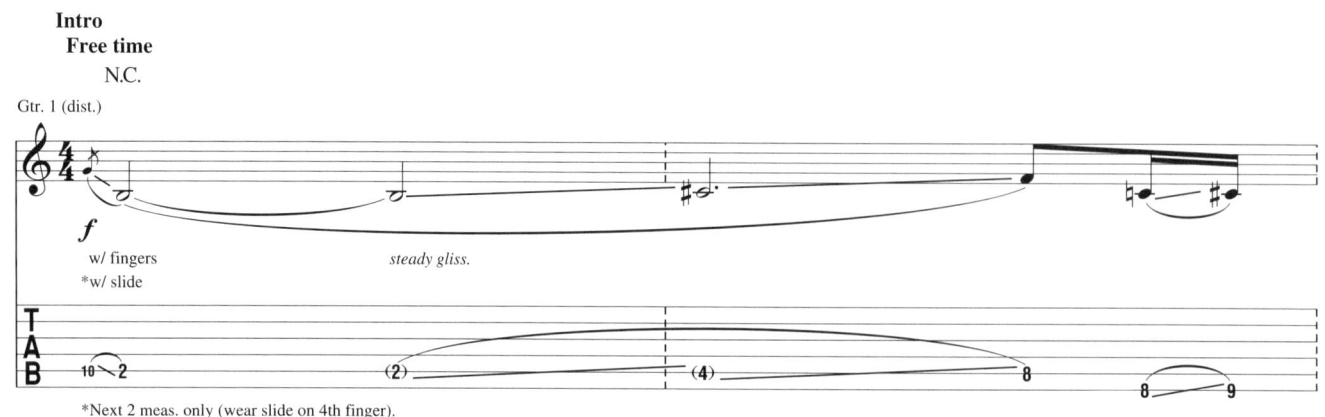

1. Well now,

Verse

yeah, _____ and I'm here ___ now, no, _____ no, _____
hold you near ___ and I whis - per in ___ your ___

Rhy. Fig. 2 _ **End Rhy. Fig. 2**

let ring

Gtr. 1: w/ Rhy. Fig. 1

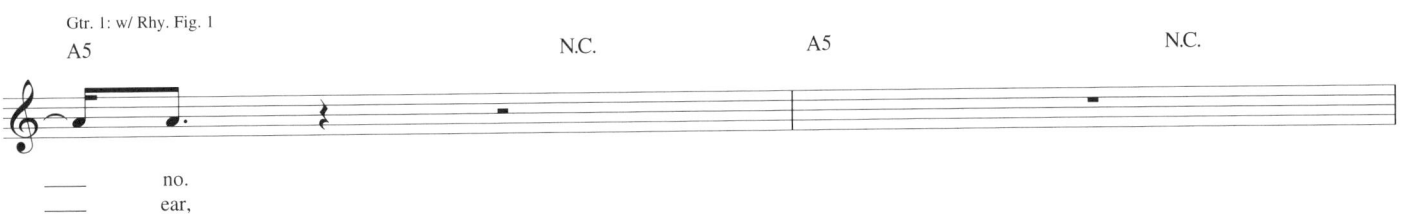

____ no.
____ ear,

And I'll
I'll ____

Gtr. 1

let ring _ _ _ _ _ _ _ _ _ _ _ _ _ _

care for you. ___ Hey, that's all ___ I wan - na ___ do.
take your hand, ___ I will make ___ you un - der - stand.

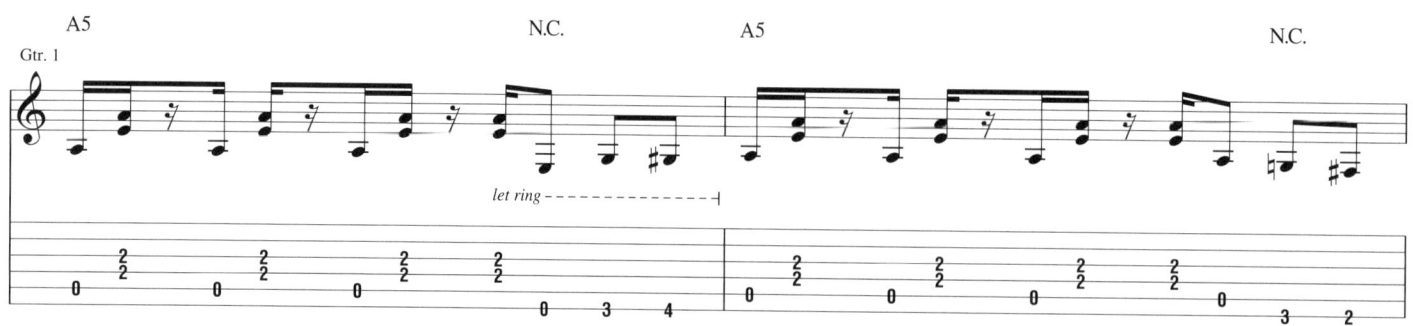

Hold ___ me, love ___ me in your ___ heart.

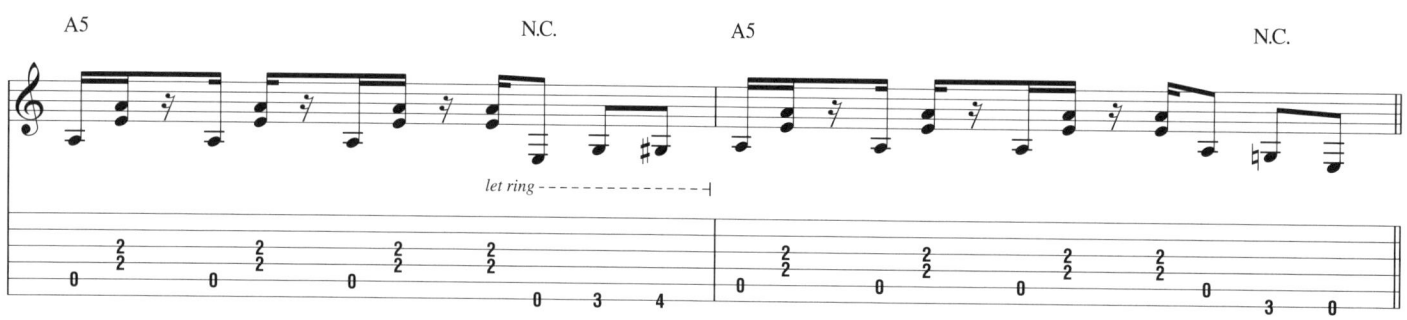

TILL I GET MY WAY

Words and Music by
Dan Auerbach and Patrick Carney

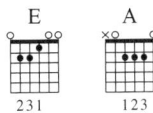

Tune up 1 step:
(low to high:) F♯-B-E-A-C♯-F♯

Intro
Moderate Rock ♩ = 116

𝄋 Verse

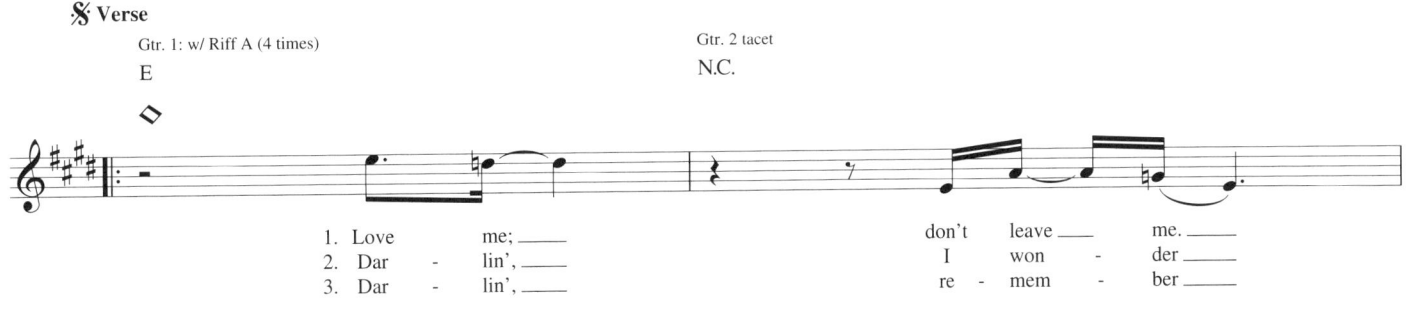

1. Love	me; ___	don't	leave ___	me. ___
2. Dar -	lin', ___	I	won -	der ___
3. Dar -	lin', ___	re - mem -	ber ___	

Make me — feel — you need — me. —
how you — pulled — me un - der. —
the cold, cold — nights — in De - cem - ber. —
You kill me —

and thrill me. — Don't you — know — that I will — be

To Coda ⊕

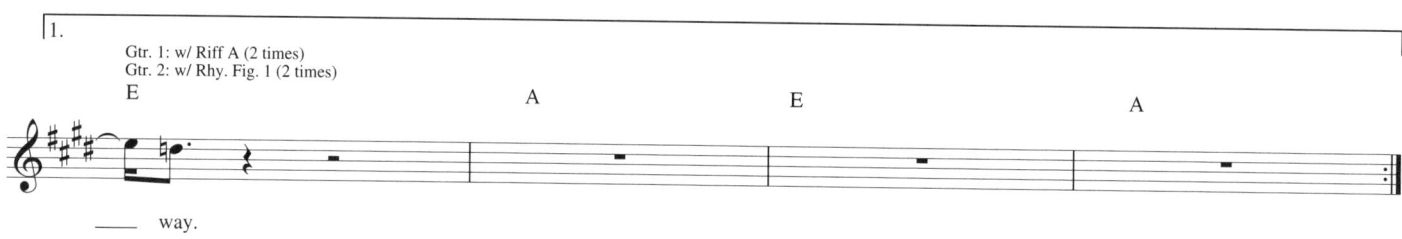

call - ing on you ev - 'ry day till I get my —

Gtr. 1

1.
Gtr. 1: w/ Riff A (2 times)
Gtr. 2: w/ Rhy. Fig. 1 (2 times)
E   A   E   A

— way.

2.
Gtr. 1: w/ Riff A (2 times)
Gtr. 2: w/ Rhy. Fig. 1 (2 times)
E   A   E   A

— way, till I get — my way. _____

Guitar Solo
        E
Gtr. 2

Gtr. 1

68

WHEN THE LIGHTS GO OUT

Words and Music by
Dan Auerbach and Patrick Carney

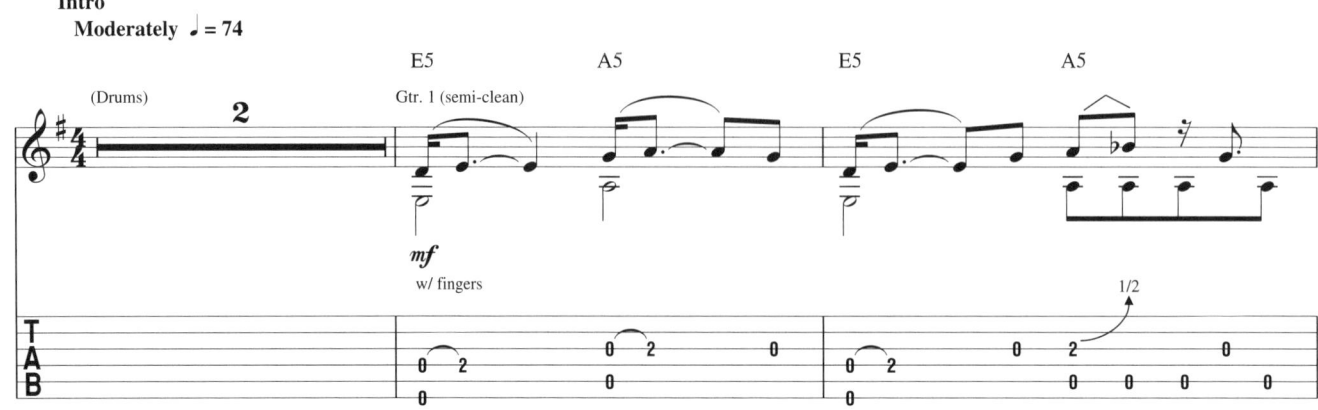

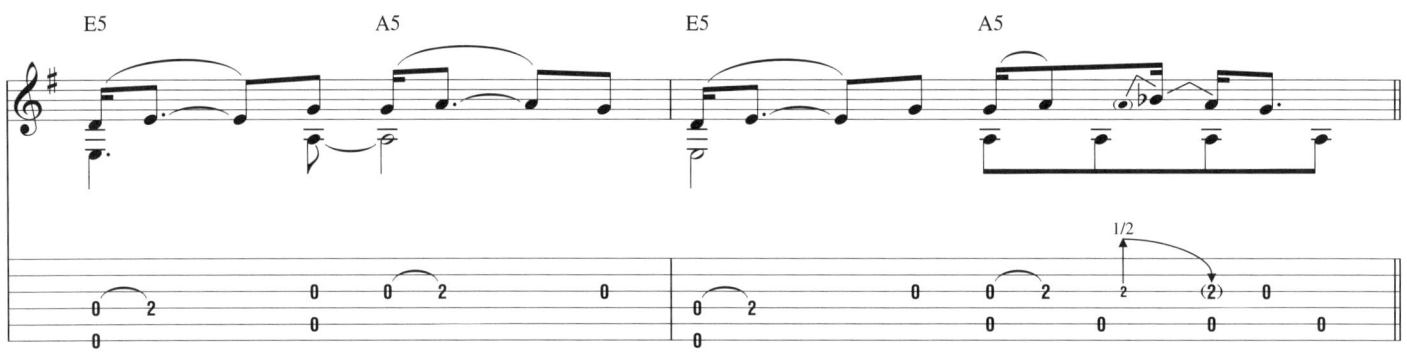

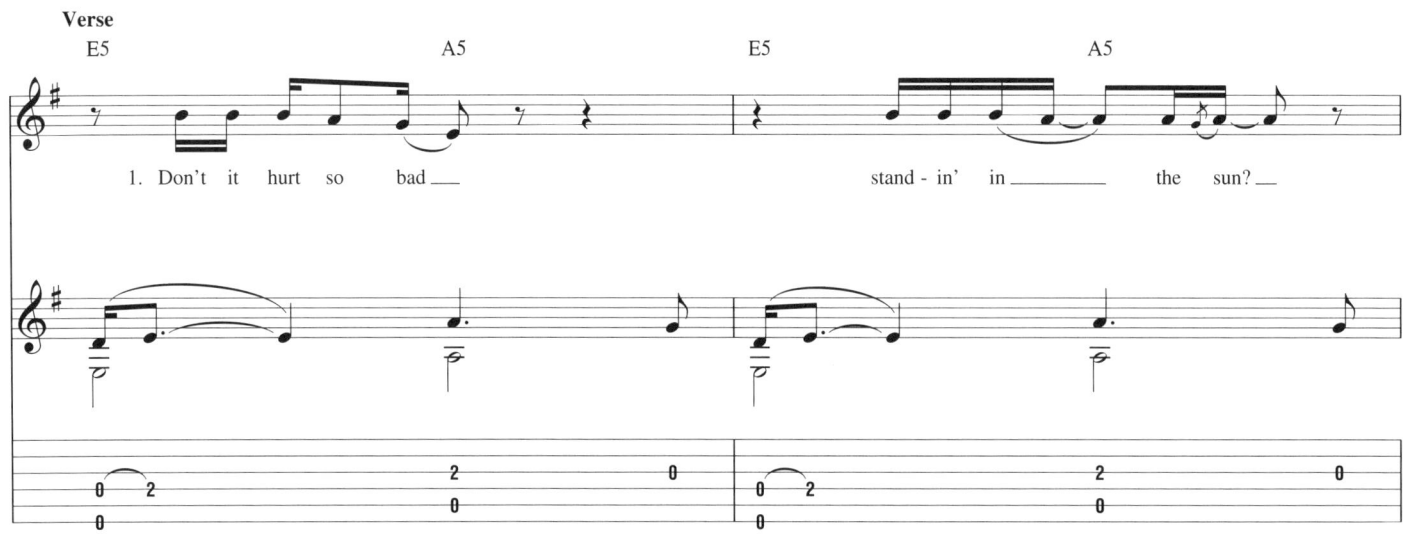

1. Don't it hurt so bad ___ stand - in' in ___ the sun? ___

𝄋 Verse

2. What a way ___ to live, ___ back of your _____ class.
3. See the moon, see the stars

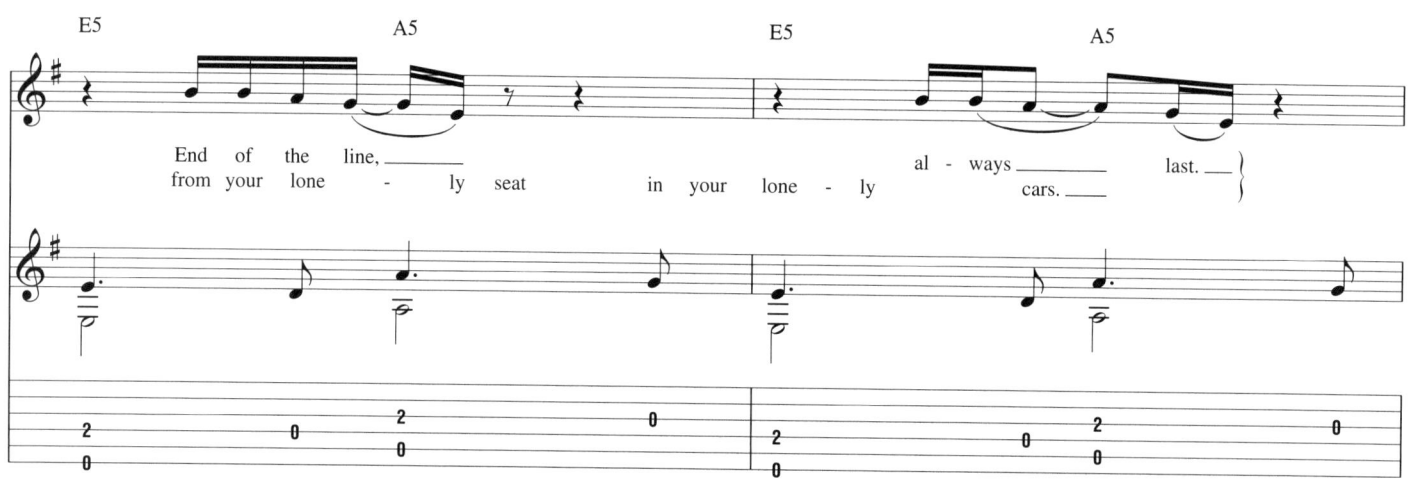

End of the line, _____ al - ways _____ last. ___
from your lone - ly seat in your lone - ly cars. ___

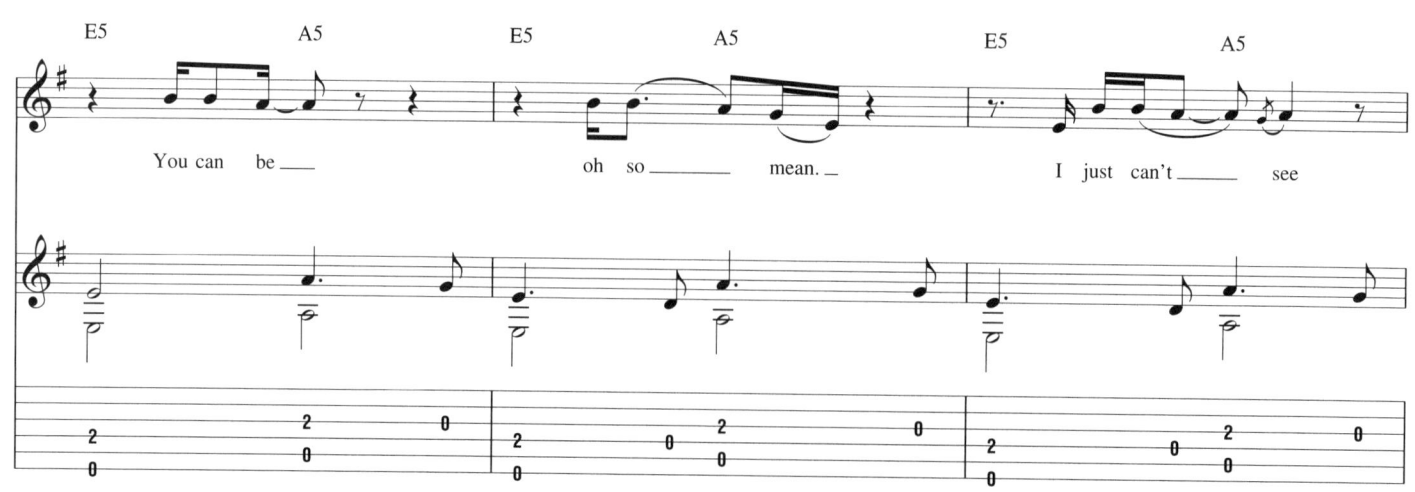

You can be ___ oh so _____ mean. ___ I just can't _____ see

72

no in be - tween.___ You know what the sun's all a - bout when the

lights go out.___

D.S. al Coda

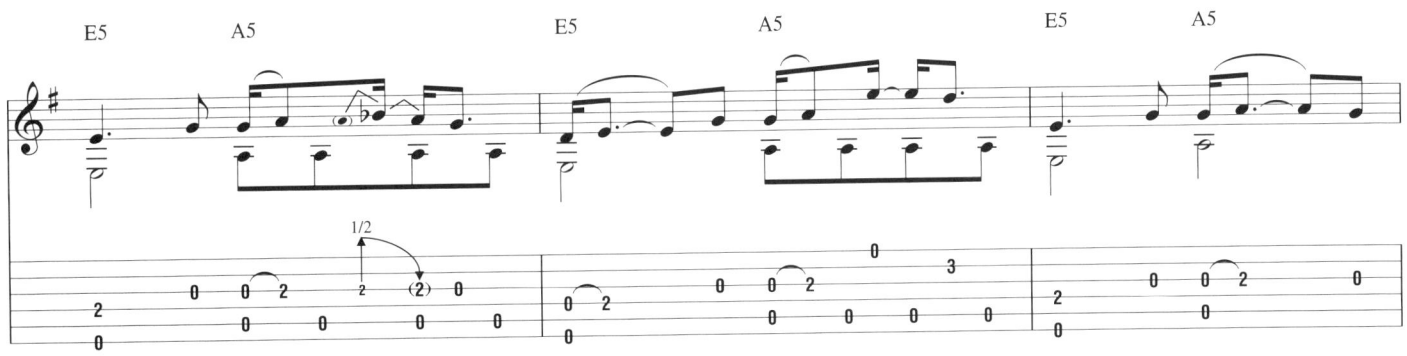

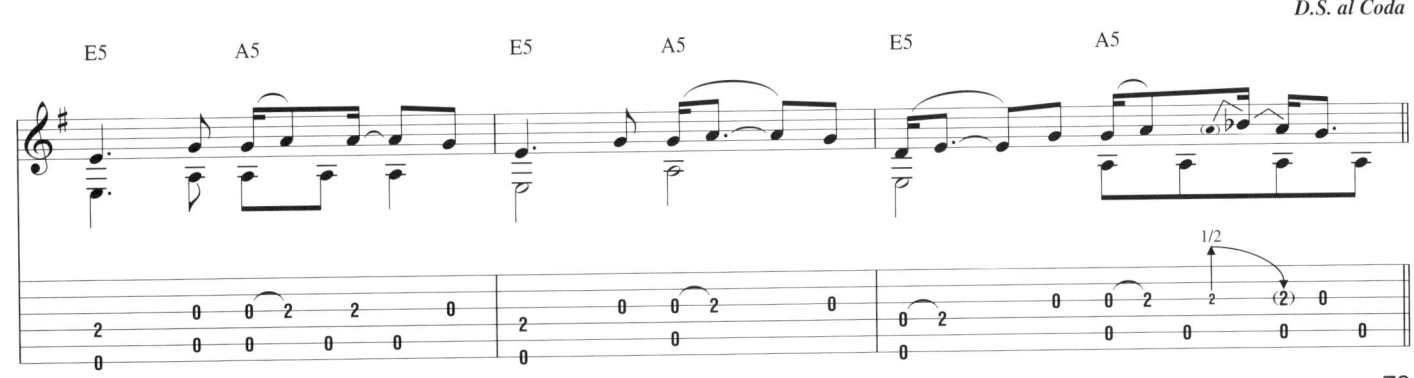

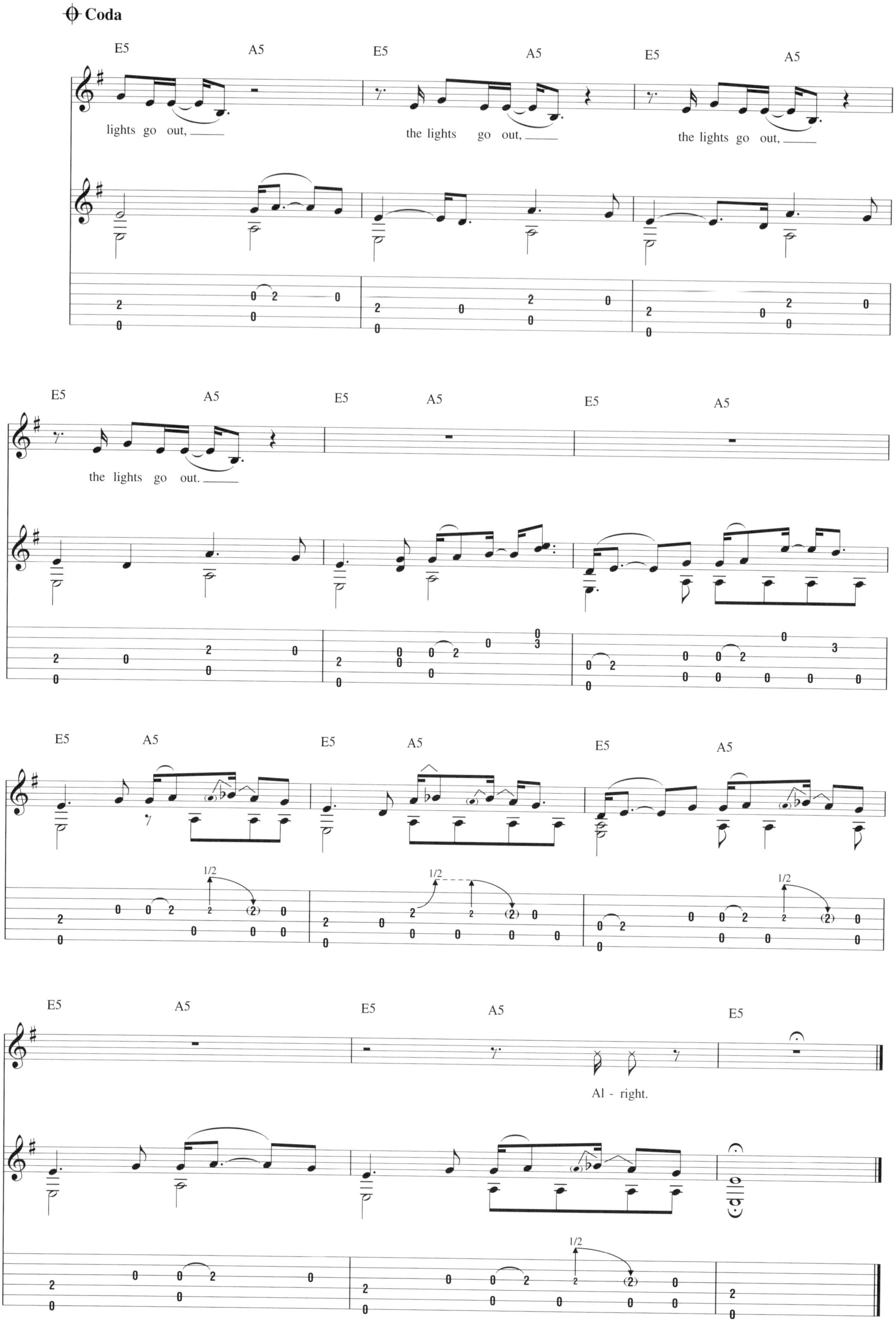
Coda
E5 A5 E5 A5 E5 A5
lights go out,
the lights go out,
the lights go out,
E5 A5 E5 A5 E5 A5
the lights go out.
E5 A5 E5 A5 E5 A5
1/2
1/2
1/2
E5 A5 E5 A5 E5
Al - right.
1/2

YOUR TOUCH

Words and Music by
Dan Auerbach and Patrick Carney

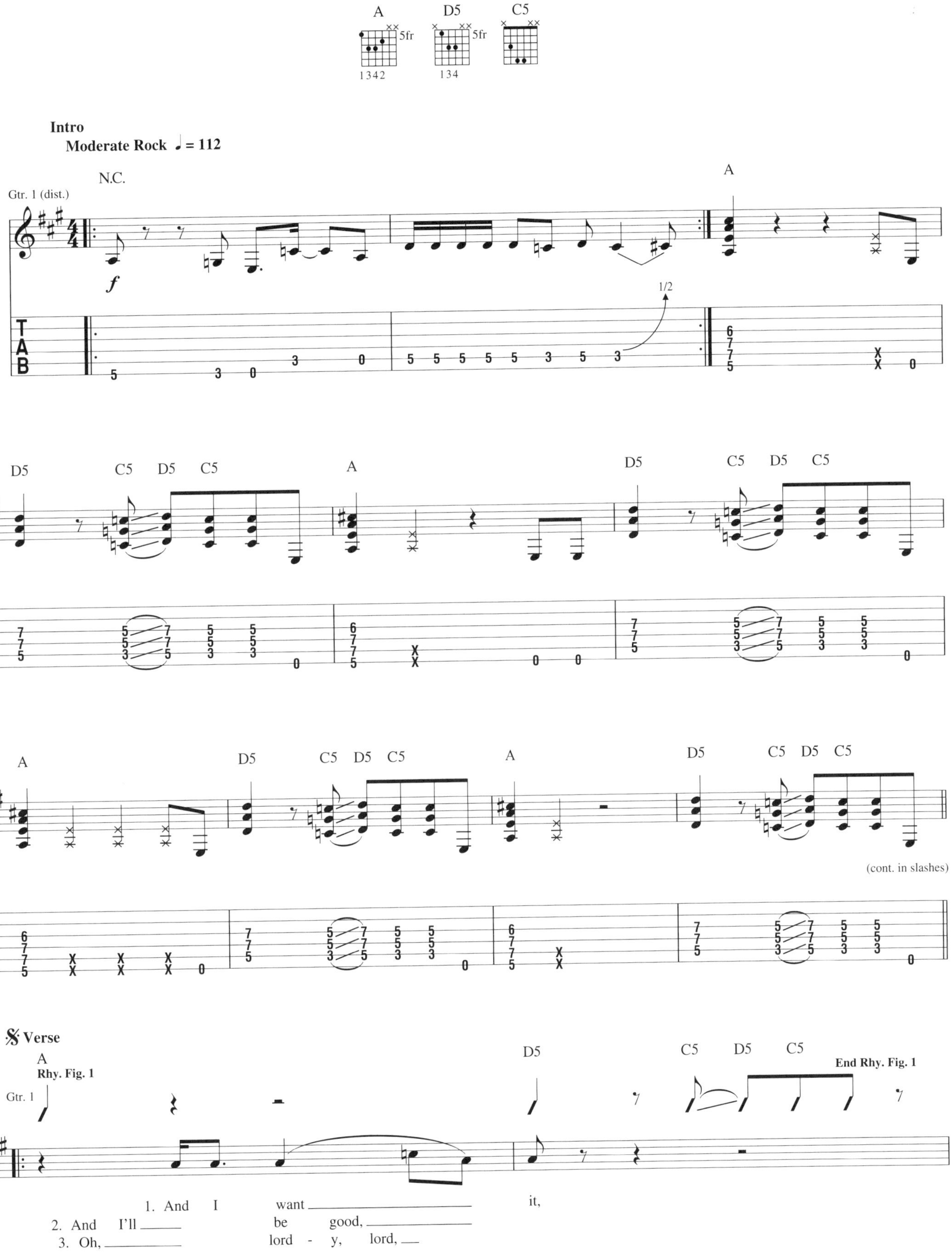
A
D5
C5
5fr
1342
134
Intro
Moderate Rock ♩ = 112
N.C.
Gtr. 1 (dist.)
1/2
(cont. in slashes)
Verse
Rhy. Fig. 1
End Rhy. Fig. 1
Gtr. 1
1. And I want ___ it,
2. And I'll ___ be good, ___
3. Oh, ___ lord - y, lord, ___

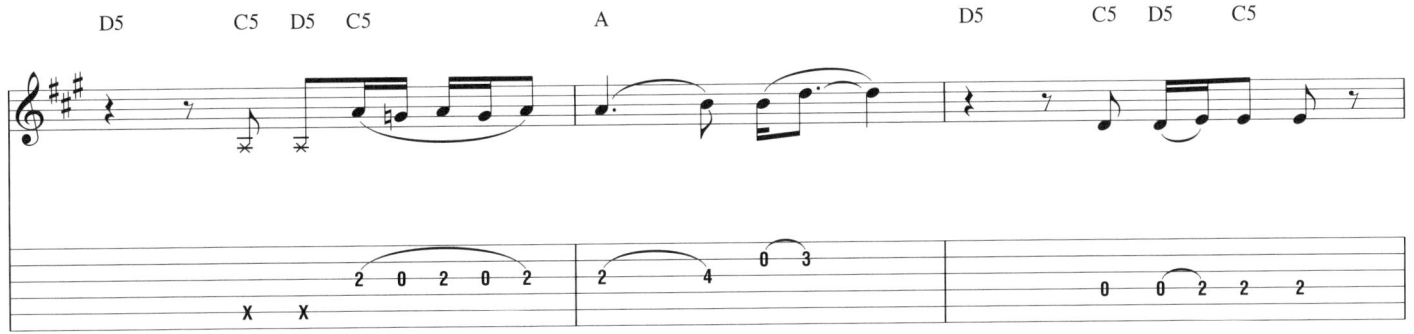

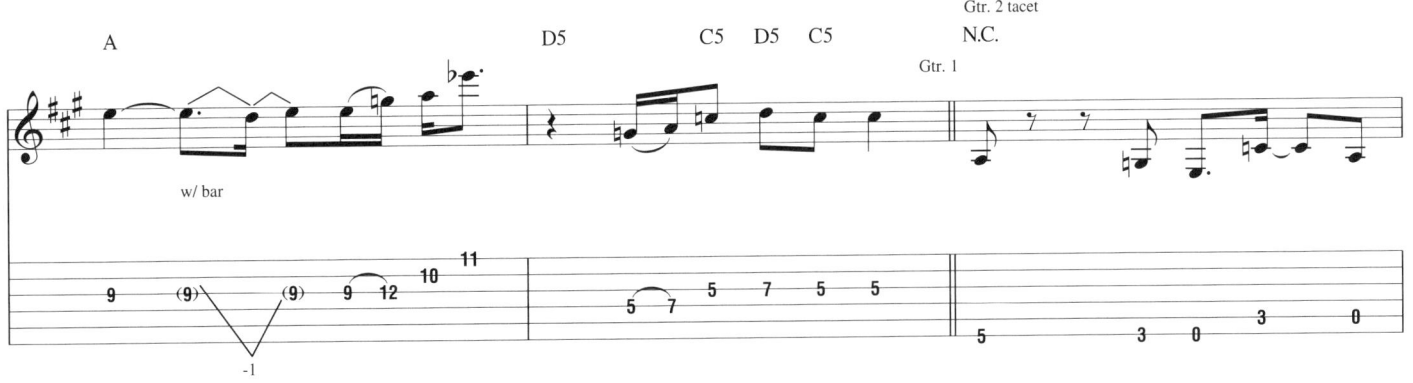

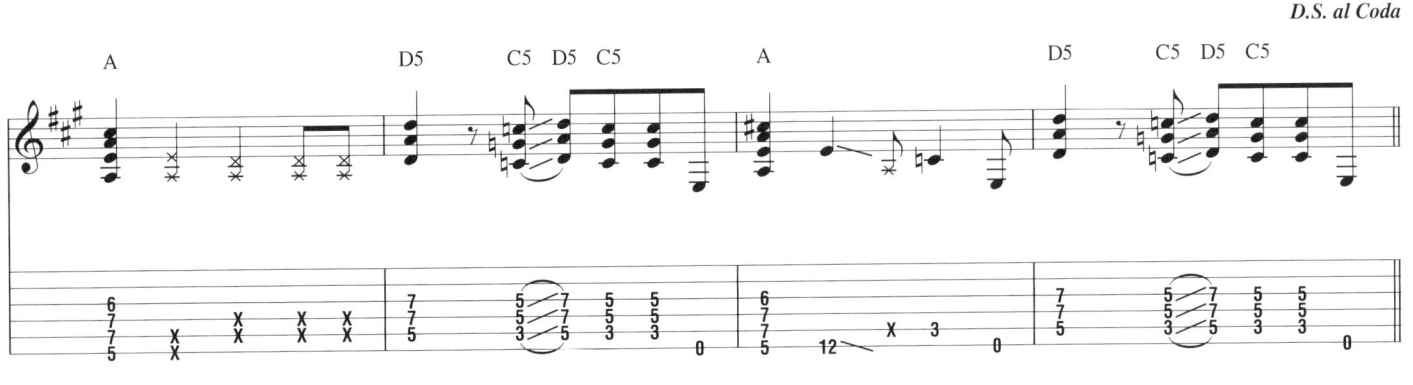

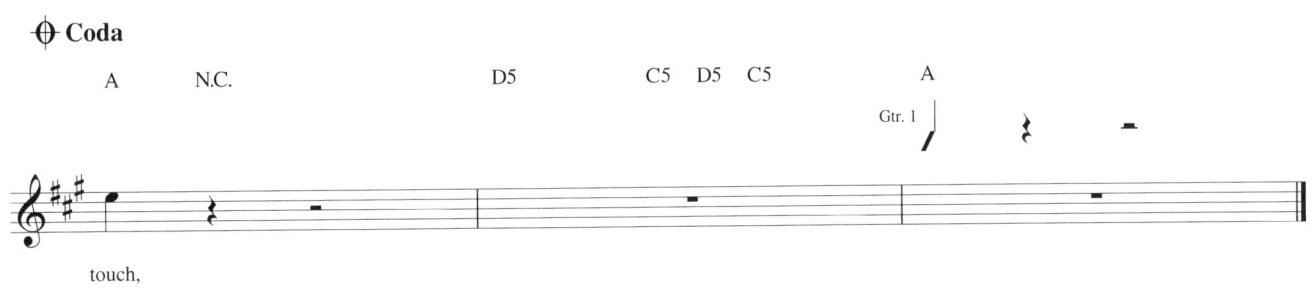

touch,

GUITAR NOTATION LEGEND

Guitar music can be notated three different ways: on a *musical staff*, in *tablature*, and in *rhythm slashes*.

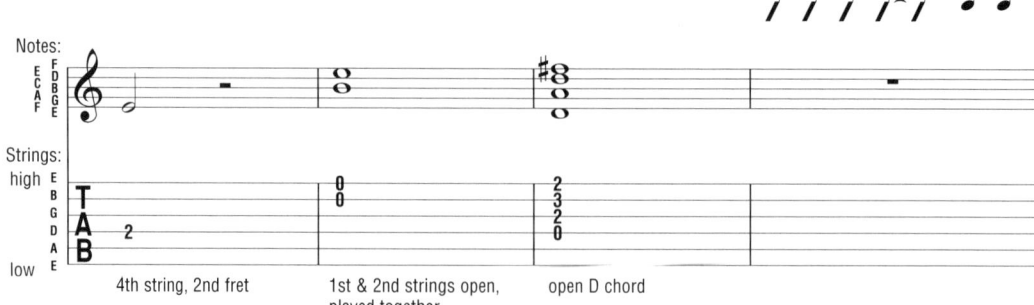

RHYTHM SLASHES are written above the staff. Strum chords in the rhythm indicated. Use the chord diagrams found at the top of the first page of the transcription for the appropriate chord voicings. Round noteheads indicate single notes.

THE MUSICAL STAFF shows pitches and rhythms and is divided by bar lines into measures. Pitches are named after the first seven letters of the alphabet.

TABLATURE graphically represents the guitar fingerboard. Each horizontal line represents a string, and each number represents a fret.

HALF-STEP BEND: Strike the note and bend up 1/2 step.

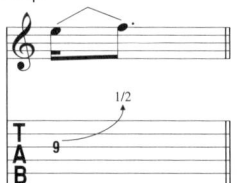

WHOLE-STEP BEND: Strike the note and bend up one step.

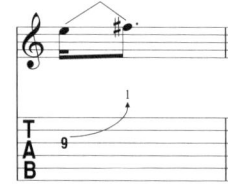

GRACE NOTE BEND: Strike the note and immediately bend up as indicated.

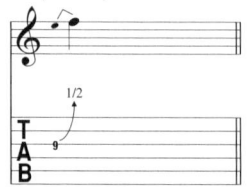

SLIGHT (MICROTONE) BEND: Strike the note and bend up 1/4 step.

BEND AND RELEASE: Strike the note and bend up as indicated, then release back to the original note. Only the first note is struck.

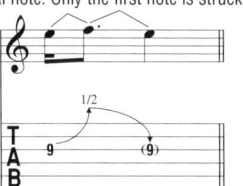

PRE-BEND: Bend the note as indicated, then strike it.

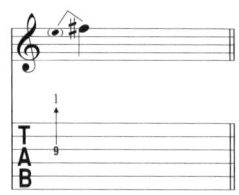

VIBRATO: The string is vibrated by rapidly bending and releasing the note with the fretting hand.

WIDE VIBRATO: The pitch is varied to a greater degree by vibrating with the fretting hand.

HAMMER-ON: Strike the first (lower) note with one finger, then sound the higher note (on the same string) with another finger by fretting it without picking.

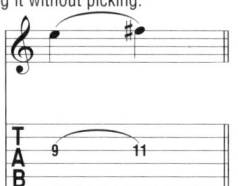

PULL-OFF: Place both fingers on the notes to be sounded. Strike the first note and without picking, pull the finger off to sound the second (lower) note.

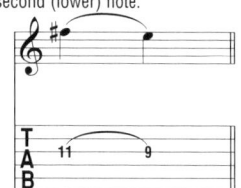

LEGATO SLIDE: Strike the first note and then slide the same fret-hand finger up or down to the second note. The second note is not struck.

SHIFT SLIDE: Same as legato slide, except the second note is struck.

TRILL: Very rapidly alternate between the notes indicated by continuously hammering on and pulling off.

TAPPING: Hammer ("tap") the fret indicated with the pick-hand index or middle finger and pull off to the note fretted by the fret hand.

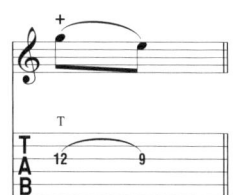

NATURAL HARMONIC: Strike the note while the fret-hand lightly touches the string directly over the fret indicated.

PINCH HARMONIC: The note is fretted normally and a harmonic is produced by adding the edge of the thumb or the tip of the index finger of the pick hand to the normal pick attack.

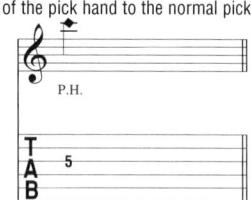

PICK SCRAPE: The edge of the pick is rubbed down (or up) the string, producing a scratchy sound.

MUFFLED STRINGS: A percussive sound is produced by laying the fret hand across the string(s) without depressing, and striking them with the pick hand.

PALM MUTING: The note is partially muted by the pick hand lightly touching the string(s) just before the bridge.

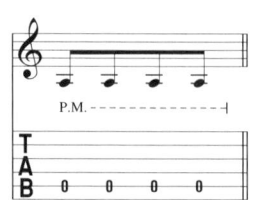

RAKE: Drag the pick across the strings indicated with a single motion.

TREMOLO PICKING: The note is picked as rapidly and continuously as possible.

VIBRATO BAR DIVE AND RETURN: The pitch of the note or chord is dropped a specified number of steps (in rhythm), then returned to the original pitch.

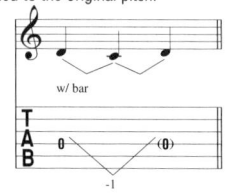

VIBRATO BAR SCOOP: Depress the bar just before striking the note, then quickly release the bar.

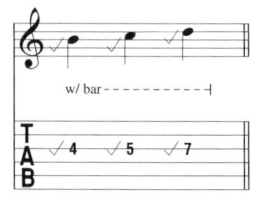

VIBRATO BAR DIP: Strike the note and then immediately drop a specified number of steps, then release back to the original pitch.

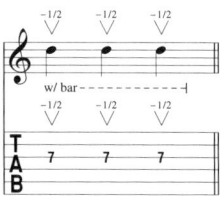

Great **DVD** selections from **CHERRY LANE**

DVD

Alternate Tuning for the Hard Rock Guitarist
taught by Rick Plunkett
02501457 DVD $19.99

Beginning Blues Guitar
RHYTHM AND SOLOS
taught by Al Ek
02501325 DVD $19.99

Black Label Society
featuring Danny Gill
Guitar Legendary Licks
02500983 2-DVD Set $29.95

Black Sabbath
featuring Danny Gill
Guitar Legendary Licks
02500874 DVD $24.95

Blues Masters by the Bar
taught by Dave Celentano
02501146 DVD $24.99

Children of Bodom
ALEXI LAIHO'S LEGENDARY LICKS
taught by Danny Gill
02501398 DVD $24.99

Classical Guitar Favorites
featuring Danny Gill
Guitar Legendary Licks
02500899 DVD $24.95

John Denver
featuring Nate LaPointe
Guitar Legendary Licks
02500917 DVD $24.95

Learn to Play the Songs of Bob Dylan
taught by Nate LaPointe
Guitar Legendary Licks
02500918 DVD $24.95

Funky Rhythm Guitar
taught by Buzz Feiten
02501393 DVD $24.99

Grateful Dead — Classic Songs
featuring Nate LaPointe
Guitar Legendary Licks
02500968 DVD $24.95

Grateful Dead
featuring Nate LaPointe
Guitar Legendary Licks
02500551 DVD $24.95

Guitar Heroes
taught by Danny Gill
Guitar Legendary Licks
02501069 2-DVD Set $29.95

Home Recording Presents: Miking Guitars in the Studio
featuring Steven Lee
02500629 DVD $24.95

Learn Rock Harmonica
taught by Al Ek
02501393 DVD $24.99

Life of the Party
PLAY PIANO IN AN INSTANT
by Bill Gulino
Hosted by John Sebastian
02500725 Book/CD/DVD Pack $49.95

Metallica – 1983-1988
featuring Doug Boduch
Bass Legendary Licks
02500481 DVD $24.95

Metallica – 1988-1997
featuring Doug Boduch
Bass Legendary Licks
02500484 DVD $24.95

Metallica – 1983-1988
featuring Nathan Kilen
Drum Legendary Licks
02500482 DVD $24.95

Metallica – 1988-1997
featuring Nathan Kilen
Drum Legendary Licks
02500485 DVD $24.95

Metallica – 1983-1988
featuring Doug Boduch
Guitar Legendary Licks
02500479 DVD $24.95

Metallica – 1988-1997
featuring Doug Boduch
Guitar Legendary Licks
02500480 DVD $24.95

Metallica: Classic Songs
featuring Danny Gill
Bass Legendary Licks
02500841 DVD $24.95

Metallica: Classic Songs
featuring Jack E. Roth
Drum Legendary Licks
02500839 DVD $24.95

Metallica: Classic Songs
featuring Danny Gill
Guitar Legendary Licks
02500840 DVD $24.95

Modes for the Rock Guitarists
taught by Dave Celentano
02501449 DVD $19.99

Home Recording Magazine's 100 Recording Tips and Tricks
STRATEGIES AND SOLUTIONS FOR YOUR HOME STUDIO
02500509 DVD $19.95

Ozzy Osbourne – The Randy Rhoads Years
featuring Danny Gill
Guitar Legendary Licks
02501301 2-DVD Set $29.99

Pink Floyd – Learn the Songs from Dark Side of the Moon
by Nate LaPointe
Guitar Legendary Licks
02500919 DVD $24.95

Poncho Sanchez
featuring the Poncho Sanchez Latin Jazz Band
02500729 DVD $24.95

Joe Satriani
featuring Danny Gill
Guitar Legendary Licks Series
02500767 2-DVD Set $29.95

Joe Satriani – Classic Songs
featuring Danny Gill
Guitar Legendary Licks
02500913 2-DVD Set $29.95

The Latin Funk Connection
02501417 DVD $24.99

Johnny Winter
taught by Al Ek
Guitar Legendary Licks
02501307 2-DVD Set 29.95

Johnny Winter
SLIDE GUITAR
featuring Johnny Winter with instruction by Al Ek
Guitar Legendary Licks
02501042 DVD $29.95

Wolfmother
featuring Danny Gill
02501062 DVD $24.95

See your local music retailer or contact

7777 W. BLUEMOUND RD. P.O. BOX 13819 MILWAUKEE, WI 53213

0909

THE HOTTEST TAB SONGBOOKS AVAILABLE FOR GUITAR & BASS!

PLAY IT LIKE IT IS GUITAR WITH TABLATURE — NOTE-FOR-NOTE TRANSCRIPTIONS

PLAY IT LIKE IT IS BASS WITH TABLATURE — NOTE-FOR-NOTE TRANSCRIPTIONS

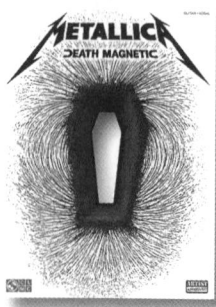

from

cherry lane music company

For complete listing of Cherry Lane titles available, including contents listings, please visit our website at **www.cherrylane.com**

Guitar Transcriptions

02500702 Best of Black Label Society	$22.95
02500842 Black Label Society – Mafia	$19.95
02500116 Black Sabbath – Riff by Riff	$14.95
02500882 Blues Masters by the Bar	$19.95
02500921 Best of Joe Bonamassa	$22.95
02501272 Bush – 16 Stone	$21.95
02500179 Mary Chapin Carpenter Authentic Guitar Style of	$16.95
02500336 Eric Clapton – Just the Riffs	$12.99
02506319 Eric Clapton – Riff by Riff	$17.95
02500684 Dashboard Confessional – A Mark • A Mission • A Brand • A Scar	$19.95
02500689 Dashboard Confessional – The Places You Have Come to Fear the Most	$17.95
02500843 Dashboard Confessional – The Swiss Army Romance	$17.95
02506878 John Denver Anthology for Easy Guitar Revised Edition	$15.95
02506901 John Denver Authentic Guitar Style	$14.95
02500984 John Denver – Folk Singer	$19.95
02506928 John Denver – Greatest Hits for Fingerstyle Guitar	$14.95
02500632 John Denver Collection Strum & Sing Series	$9.95
02500652 Dio – 5 of the Best	$9.95
02500607 The Best of Dispatch	$19.95
02501147 50 Easy Spanish Guitar Solos	$14.95
02500198 Best of Foreigner	$19.95
02500990 Donavon Frankenreiter	$19.95
02501242 Guns N' Roses – Anthology	$24.95
02506953 Guns N' Roses – Appetite for Destruction	$22.95
02501286 Guns N' Roses Complete, Volume 1	$24.95
02501287 Guns N' Roses Complete, Volume 2	$24.95
02506211 Guns N' Roses – 5 of the Best, Vol. 1	$12.95
02506975 Guns N' Roses – GN'R Lies	$19.95
02500299 Guns N' Roses – Live Era '87-'93 Highlights	$24.95
02501193 Guns N' Roses – Use Your Illusion I	$24.95
02501194 Guns N' Roses – Use Your Illusion II	$24.95
02506325 Metallica – The Art of Kirk Hammett	$17.95
02500939 Hawthorne Heights – The Silence in Black and White	$19.95
02500458 Best of Warren Haynes	$22.95
02500476 Warren Haynes – Guide to Slide Guitar	$17.95
02500387 Best of Heart	$19.95
02500016 The Art of James Hetfield	$17.95
02500007 Hole – Celebrity Skin	$19.95
02500873 Jazz for the Blues Guitarist	$14.95
02500554 Jack Johnson – Brushfire Fairytales	$19.95
02500831 Jack Johnson – In Between Dreams	$19.95
02500653 Jack Johnson – On and On	$19.95

02500858 Jack Johnson – Strum & Sing	$10.95
02500380 Lenny Kravitz – Greatest Hits	$19.95
02500024 Best of Lenny Kravitz	$19.95
02500129 Adrian Legg – Pickin' 'n' Squintin'	$19.95
02500362 Best of Little Feat	$19.95
02501094 Hooks That Kill – The Best of Mick Mars & Mötley Crüe	$19.95
02500305 Best of The Marshall Tucker Band	$19.95
02501077 Dave Matthews Band – Anthology	$24.95
02501357 Dave Matthews Band – Before These Crowded Streets	$19.95
02500553 Dave Matthews Band – Busted Stuff	$22.95
02501279 Dave Matthews Band – Crash	$19.95
02500389 Dave Matthews Band – Everyday	$19.95
02501266 Dave Matthews Band – Under the Table and Dreaming	$19.95
02500131 Dave Matthews/Tim Reynolds – Live at Luther College, Vol. 1	$19.95
02500611 Dave Matthews/Tim Reynolds – Live at Luther College, Vol. 2	$22.95
02500986 John Mayer – Continuum	$22.95
02500705 John Mayer – Heavier Things	$22.95
02500529 John Mayer – Room for Squares	$22.95
02506965 Metallica – ...And Justice for All	$22.95
02501267 Metallica – Death Magnetic	$24.95
02506210 Metallica – 5 of the Best/Vol.1	$12.95
02506235 Metallica – 5 of the Best/Vol. 2	$12.95
02500070 Metallica – Garage, Inc.	$24.95
02507018 Metallica – Kill 'Em All	$19.95
02501232 Metallica – Live: Binge & Purge	$19.95
02501275 Metallica – Load	$24.95
02507920 Metallica – Master of Puppets	$19.95
02501195 Metallica – Metallica	$22.95
02501297 Metallica – ReLoad	$24.95
02507019 Metallica – Ride the Lightning	$19.95
02500279 Metallica – S&M Highlights	$24.95
02500638 Metallica – St. Anger	$24.95
02500577 Molly Hatchet – 5 of the Best	$9.95
02500846 Best of Steve Morse Band and Dixie Dregs	$19.95
02500765 Jason Mraz – Waiting for My Rocket to Come	$19.95
02500448 Best of Ted Nugent	$19.95
02500707 Ted Nugent – Legendary Licks	$19.95
02500844 Best of O.A.R. (Of a Revolution)	$22.95
02500348 Ozzy Osbourne – Blizzard of Ozz	$19.95
02501277 Ozzy Osbourne – Diary of a Madman	$19.95
02507904 Ozzy Osbourne/Randy Rhoads Tribute	$22.95
02500524 The Bands of Ozzfest	$16.95
02500525 More Bands of Ozzfest	$16.95
02500680 Don't Stop Believin': The Steve Perry Anthology	$22.95

02500025 Primus Anthology – A-N (Guitar/Bass)	$19.95
02500091 Primus Anthology – O-Z (Guitar/Bass)	$19.95
02500468 Primus – Sailing the Seas of Cheese	$19.95
02500875 Queens of the Stone Age – Lullabies to Paralyze	$24.95
02500608 Queens of the Stone Age – Songs for the Deaf	$19.95
02500659 The Best of Bonnie Raitt	$24.95
02501268 Joe Satriani	$22.95
02501299 Joe Satriani – Crystal Planet	$24.95
02500306 Joe Satriani – Engines of Creation	$22.95
02501205 Joe Satriani – The Extremist	$22.95
02507029 Joe Satriani – Flying in a Blue Dream	$22.95
02501155 Joe Satriani – Professor Satchafunkilus and the Musterion of Rock	$24.95
02500544 Joe Satriani – Strange Beautiful Music	$22.95
02500920 Joe Satriani – Super Colossal	$22.95
02506959 Joe Satriani – Surfing with the Alien	$19.95
02500560 Joe Satriani Anthology	$24.95
02501255 Best of Joe Satriani	$19.95
02501238 Sepultura – Chaos A.D.	$19.95
02500188 Best of the Brian Setzer Orchestra	$19.95
02500985 Sex Pistols – Never Mind the Bollocks, Here's the Sex Pistols	$19.95
02501230 Soundgarden – Superunknown	$19.95
02500799 Tenacious D	$19.95
02501035 Tenacious D – The Pick of Destiny	$19.95
02501263 Tesla – Time's Making Changes	$19.95
02501147 30 Easy Spanish Guitar Solos	$14.95
02500561 Learn Funk Guitar with Tower of Power's Jeff Tamelier	$19.95
02501007 Keith Urban – Love, Pain & The Whole Crazy Thing	$24.95
02500636 The White Stripes – Elephant	$19.95
02501095 The White Stripes – Icky Thump	$19.95
02500583 The White Stripes – White Blood Cells	$19.95
02501092 Wilco – Sky Blue Sky	$22.95
02500431 Best of Johnny Winter	$19.95
02500949 Wolfmother	$22.95
02500199 Best of Zakk Wylde	$22.95
02500700 Zakk Wylde – Legendary Licks	$19.95

Bass Transcriptions

02501108 Bass Virtuosos	$19.95
02500117 Black Sabbath – Riff by Riff Bass	$17.95
02506966 Guns N' Roses – Appetite for Destruction	$19.95
02500639 Metallica – St. Anger	$19.95
02500771 Best of Rancid for Bass	$17.95
02501120 Best of Tower of Power for Bass	$19.95
02500317 Victor Wooten Songbook	$22.95

Transcribed Scores

02500424 The Best of Metallica	$24.95
02500715 Mr. Big – Greatest Hits	$24.95
02500883 Mr. Big – Lean into It	$24.95

See your local music dealer or contact:

cherry lane music company

EXCLUSIVELY DISTRIBUTED BY
HAL•LEONARD CORPORATION
7777 W. BLUEMOUND RD. P.O. BOX 13819 MILWAUKEE, WI 53213

Prices, contents, and availability subject to change without notice.

0909